Max Lucado

GOD CAME NEAR

JANUARY 1

All the splendor of heaven revealed in a human body. For a period ever so brief, the doors to the throne room were open and God came near. His Majesty was seen. Heaven touched the earth and, as a result, earth can know heaven.

GOD CAME NEAR, P. 7

Jesus answered..."Anyone who has seen me has seen the Father."

JOHN 14:9

DECEMBER 31

J esus' love does not depend upon what we do for him. Not at all. In the eyes of the King, you have value simply because you are. You don't have to look nice or perform well. Your value is inborn. Period.

NO WONDER THEY CALL HIM THE SAVIOR, P. 3

God said, "Let us make man in our image, in our likeness."

GENESIS 1:26

JANUARY 2

L ook at the Messiah himself. A blue-collar Jew whose claim
altered a world and whose promise has never been equaled.

NO WONDER THEY CALL HIM THE SAVIOR, P. 14

I am the light of the world. Whoever follows me will never walk in
darkness, but will have the light of life.

JOHN 8:12

DECEMBER 30

In the cellar of your heart lurk the ghosts of yesterday's sins. Sins you've confessed; errors of which you've repented; damage you've done your best to repair.... Do yourself a favor. Purge your cellar. Exorcise your basement. Take the Roman nails of Calvary and board up the door. And remember...he forgot.

GOD CAME NEAR, PP. 50,51

God did not send his Son into the world to condemn the world, but to save the world through him.

JOHN 3:17

JANUARY 3

Why did he pick you? He wanted to. After all, you are his. He made you. He brought you home. He owns you. And once upon a time, he tapped you on the shoulder and reminded you of that fact. No matter how long you'd waited or how much time you'd wasted, you are his and he has a place for you.

<small>AND THE ANGELS WERE SILENT</small>

I have other sheep that are not of this sheep pen. I must bring them also. They too will listen to my voice, and there shall be one flock and one shepherd.

<small>JOHN 10:16</small>

DECEMBER 29

Remember, Paul begged, remember Jesus. Before you remember anything, remember him. If you forget anything, don't forget him. Oh, but how quickly we forget. So much happens through the years.... And, somewhere, back there, we leave him. We don't turn away from him...we just don't take him with us. Assignments come. Promotions come. Budgets are made. Kids are born, and the Christ...the Christ is forgotten.

SIX HOURS ONE FRIDAY, P. 76

Let us fix our eyes on Jesus, the author and perfecter of our faith, who for the joy set before him endured the cross.... Consider him.

HEBREWS 12:2,3

JANUARY 4

God, motivated by love and directed by divinity, surprised everyone. He became a man. In an untouchable mystery, he disguised himself as a carpenter and lived in a dusty Judean village. Determined to prove his love for his creation, he walked incognito through his own world. His calloused hands touched wounds and his compassionate tongue touched hearts. He became one of us.

No Wonder They Call Him the Savior, p. 57

He went around doing good and healing all who were under the power of the devil, because God was with him.

Acts 10:38

DECEMBER 28

The magical dust of Christmas glittered on the cheeks of humanity ever so briefly, reminding us of what is worth having and what we were intended to be. We forgot our compulsion with winning, wooing, and warring. We hung up our stopwatches and weapons. We stepped off our racetracks and roller coasters and looked outward toward the star of Bethlehem.

GOD CAME NEAR, P. 22

The star they had seen in the east went ahead of them until it stopped over the place where the child was.... They bowed down and worshiped him.

MATTHEW 2:9,11

JANUARY 5

For those who know the Author of Life, death is nothing more than Satan's dead-man's-bluff.

GOD CAME NEAR, P. 28

Then [Jesus] went up and touched the coffin, and those carrying it stood still. He said, "Young man, I say to you, get up!" The dead man sat up and began to talk.

LUKE 7:14,15

DECEMBER 27

The people would scoff at anyone who told them the Messiah lay in the arms of a teenager on the outskirts of their village. They were all too busy to consider the possibility. Those who missed His Majesty's arrival that night missed it not because of evil acts or malice; no, they missed it because they simply weren't looking. Little has changed in the last two thousand years, has it?

GOD CAME NEAR, P. 11

He came unto his own, and his own received him not.

JOHN 1:11

JANUARY 6

God is the shepherd in search of his lamb. His legs are scratched, his feet are sore and his eyes are burning. He scales the cliffs and traverses the fields. He explores the caves. He cups his hands to his mouth and calls into the canyon. And the name he calls is yours.

AND THE ANGELS WERE SILENT

Suppose one of you has a hundred sheep and loses one of them. Does he not leave the ninety-nine in the open country and go after the lost sheep until he finds it?

LUKE 15:4

DECEMBER 26

God became a man. While the creatures of earth walked unaware, Divinity arrived. Heaven opened herself and placed her most precious one in a human womb.

GOD CAME NEAR, P. 12

The Word became flesh and lived for a while among us.

JOHN 1:14

JANUARY 7

Warning. Something happens to a person who has witnessed His Majesty. He becomes addicted. One glimpse of the King and you are consumed by a desire to see more of him and say more about him.

GOD CAME NEAR, P. 7

Yours, O LORD is the greatness and the power and the glory and the majesty and the splendor, for everything in heaven and earth is yours.

1 CHRONICLES 29:11

DECEMBER 25

This baby had overlooked the universe. These rags keeping him warm were the robes of eternity. His golden throne room had been abandoned in favor of a dirty sheep pen. And worshiping angels had been replaced with kind but bewildered shepherds.

GOD CAME NEAR, P. 11

The Son is the radiance of God's glory and the exact representation of his being, sustaining all things by his powerful word.

HEBREWS 1:3

JANUARY 8

God must've had a blast. Painting the stripes on the zebra, hanging the stars in the sky, putting the gold in the sunset. What creativity! Stretching the neck of the giraffe, putting the flutter in the mockingbird's wings, planting the giggle in the hyena.... And then, as a finale to a brilliant performance, he made man.... A human who had the unique honor to bear the stamp, "In His Image."

No Wonder They Call Him the Savior, p. 56

God made the wild animals according to their kinds.... Then God said, "Let us make man in our image."

Genesis 1:25,26

DECEMBER 24

The city hums. The merchants are unaware that God has visited their planet. The innkeeper would never believe that he had just sent God into the cold.

GOD CAME NEAR, P. 11

There was no room for them in the inn.

LUKE 2:7

JANUARY 9

What are you doing with God's personal request that you live with him forever? That is the only decision which really matters. Whether or not you take the job transfer is not crucial. What college you choose or what profession you select is important, but not compared to where you spend eternity. That is the decision you will remember. What are you doing with his invitation?

AND THE ANGELS WERE SILENT

This day...I have set before you life and death, blessings and curses. Now choose life.

DEUTERONOMY 30:19

DECEMBER 23

Mary looks into the face of the baby. Her son. Her Lord. His Majesty. At this point in history, the human being who best understands who God is and what he is doing is a teenage girl in a smelly stable.

GOD CAME NEAR, P. 11

The angel said to her, "Do not be afraid, Mary.... You are to give him the name Jesus. He will be great and will be called the Son of the Most High.... His kingdom will never end."

LUKE 1:30-33

JANUARY 10

R isky love seizes the moment.

AND THE ANGELS WERE SILENT

Then Esther sent this reply to Mordecai: "I will go to the king, even though it is against the law. And if I perish, I perish."

ESTHER 4:15,16

DECEMBER 22

O ur heroes, as noble as they may have been, as courageous as they were, were conceived in the same stained society as you and I. Except one. There was one who claimed to come from a different place. There was one who, though he had the appearance of a man, claimed to have the origin of God. There was one who, while wearing the face of a Jew, had the image of the Creator.

AND THE ANGELS WERE SILENT

Jesus said, "You are from below; I am from above. You are of this world; I am not of this world."

JOHN 8:23

JANUARY 11

In God's book man is heading somewhere. He has an amazing destiny. We are being prepared to walk down the church aisle and become the bride of Jesus. We are going to live with him. Share the throne with him. Reign with him. We count. We are valuable. And what's more, our worth is built in! Our value is inborn.

NO WONDER THEY CALL HIM THE SAVIOR, P. 35

Let us rejoice and be glad and give him glory! For the wedding of the Lamb has come, and his bride has made herself ready.

REVELATION 19:7

DECEMBER 21

When it comes to goodies and candy, cherub cheeks and red noses, go to the North Pole. But when it comes to eternity, forgiveness, purpose and truth, go to the manger. Kneel with the shepherds. And worship the God who dared to do what man dared not dream.

AND THE ANGELS WERE SILENT

Today in the town of David a Savior has been born to you; he is Christ the Lord.

LUKE 2:11

JANUARY 12

L et's follow his sandalprints. Let's sit on the cold, hard floor of the cave in which he was born. Let's smell the sawdust of the carpentry shop. Let's hear his sandals slap the hard trails of Galilee. Let's sigh as we touch the healed sores of the leper. Let's smile as we see his compassion with the woman at the well. Let's cringe as we hear the hissing of hell's Satan.... Let's try to see him.

GOD CAME NEAR, P. 7

The Word became flesh and lived for a while among us. We have seen his glory, the glory of the one and only Son, who came from the Father, full of grace and truth.

JOHN 1:14

DECEMBER 20

For a few precious hours our heavenly yearnings intermesh and we become a chorus. A ragtag chorus of longshoremen, Boston lawyers, illegal immigrants, housewives, and a thousand other peculiar persons who are banking that Bethlehem's mystery is in reality, a reality.

GOD CAME NEAR, P. 22

The angel said to them, "Do not be afraid. I bring you good news of great joy that will be for all the people."

LUKE 2:10

JANUARY 13

Jesus offers the invitation as a penniless rabbi in an oppressed nation. He has no political office, no connections with the authorities in Rome. He hasn't written a bestseller or earned a diploma. Yet, he dares to look into the leathery faces of farmers and tired faces of housewives and offer rest.

SIX HOURS ONE FRIDAY, P. 32

Come to me, all you who are weary and burdened, and I will give you rest.

MATTHEW 11:28

DECEMBER 19

God as a fetus. Holiness sleeping in a womb. The creator of life being created. God was given eyebrows, elbows, two kidneys, and a spleen. He stretched against the walls and floated in the amniotic fluids of his mother. God had come near.

GOD CAME NEAR, P. 12

The virgin will be with child and will give birth to a son, and they will call him Immanuel—which means, "God with us."

MATTHEW 1:23

JANUARY 14

Jesus looks into the disillusioned eyes of a preacher or two from Jerusalem. He gazes into the cynical stare of a banker and the hungry eyes of a bartender and makes this paradoxical promise.

SIX HOURS ONE FRIDAY, P. 32

Jesus said, "Take my yoke upon you and learn from me, for I am gentle and humble in heart, and you will find rest for your souls."

MATTHEW 11:29

DECEMBER 18

We cannot choose the weather. We can't control the economy. We can't choose whether or not we are born with a big nose or blue eyes or a lot of hair. We can't even choose how people respond to us. But we can choose where we spend eternity. The big choice, God leaves to us.

AND THE ANGELS WERE SILENT

Everyone who calls on the name of the Lord will be saved.

ACTS 2:21

JANUARY 15

I believe God has a graciously terrible memory.... If he didn't forget, how could we pray? How could we dare enter into his presence if the moment he saw us he remembered all our pitiful past? How could we enter his throne room wearing the rags of our selfishness and gluttony? We couldn't. And we don't.... We have "put on" Christ. When God looks at us he doesn't see us; he sees Christ.

GOD CAME NEAR, P. 51

For as many of you as have been baptized into Christ have put on Christ.

GALATIANS 3:27 KJV

DECEMBER 17

Majesty in the midst of the mundane. Holiness in the filth of sheep manure and sweat. Divinity entering the world on the floor of a stable, through the womb of a teenager and in the presence of a carpenter.

GOD CAME NEAR, P. 11

[Mary] gave birth to her firstborn, a son. She wrapped him in cloths and placed him in a manger, because there was no room for them in the inn.

LUKE 2:7

JANUARY 16

We're sacrilegious not when we claim God's forgiveness, but when we allow the haunting sins of yesterday to convince us that God forgives but he doesn't forget.

GOD CAME NEAR, P. 51

Their sins and iniquities will I remember no more.

HEBREWS 10:17 KJV

DECEMBER 16

God had entered the world as a baby.... God goes to those who have time to hear him—so on this cloudless night he went to simple shepherds.

GOD CAME NEAR, P. 10

There were shepherds living out in the fields nearby, keeping watch over their flocks at night. An angel of the Lord appeared to them, and the glory of the Lord shone around them.

LUKE 2:8,9

JANUARY 17

It's the ultimate question of the Christ: Whose son is he? Is he the son of God or the sum of our dreams? Is he the force of creation or a figment of our imagination?

AND THE ANGELS WERE SILENT

"But what about you?" he asked. "Who do you say that I am?"

MATTHEW 16:15

DECEMBER 15

For our own good, Jesus demanded and demands absolute obedience. He never has had room for "almost" in his vocabulary. You are either with him or against him. With Jesus... "next time" has to become "this time." No, Jesus never had room for "almost" and he still doesn't. "Almost" may count in horseshoes and hand grenades, but with the Master, it is just as good as a "never."

No Wonder They Call Him the Savior, p. 82

Agrippa said unto Paul, "Almost thou persuadest me to be a Christian."

Acts 26:28 KJV

JANUARY 18

You are valuable just because you exist. Not because of what you do or what you have done, but simply because you are. Remember that. Remember that the next time you are left bobbing in the wake of someone's steamboat ambition. Remember that the next time some trickster tries to hang a bargain basement price tag on your self-worth.... Just think about the way Jesus honors you...and smile.

No Wonder They Call Him the Savior, p. 36

Even the very hairs of your head are all numbered.

Matthew 10:30

DECEMBER 14

I s Jesus the son of God or the sum of our dreams?... No one could ever dream a person as incredible as Jesus is. The idea...that a virgin would be selected by God to bear himself...the notion that God would don a scalp and toes and two eyes...the thought that the King of the universe would sneeze and burp and get bit by mosquitoes...it's too incredible.

AND THE ANGELS WERE SILENT

Beyond all question, the mystery of godliness is great: He appeared in a body.

1 TIMOTHY 3:16

JANUARY 19

What is the sign of the saved? Their scholarship? Their willingness to go to foreign lands? Their ability to amass an audience and preach? Their skillful pens and hope-filled volumes? Their great miracles? No. The sign of the saved is their love for the least.

AND THE ANGELS WERE SILENT

The King will reply, "I tell you the truth, whatever you did for one of the least of these brothers of mine, you did for me."

MATTHEW 25:40

DECEMBER 13

Fleshly divinity. Skin layered on spirit. Omnipotence with hair. Toenails. Knuckles. Molars. Kneecaps. Once again God walks with man.

GOD CAME NEAR, P. 37

He is the image of the invisible God, the firstborn over all creation.

COLOSSIANS 1:15

JANUARY 20

G od is an inviting God. He invited Mary to birth his son, the disciples to fish for men, the adulterous woman to start over, and Thomas to touch his wounds. God is the King who prepares the palace, sets the table, and invites his subjects to come in.

AND THE ANGELS WERE SILENT

At the time of the banquet he sent his servant to tell those who had been invited, "Come, for everything is now ready."

LUKE 14:17

DECEMBER 12

Empty throne. Spirit descending. Hushed angels. A girl...a womb...an egg. The same Divine Artist again forms a body. This time his own.

GOD CAME NEAR, P. 37

The Holy Spirit will come upon you, and the power of the Most High will overshadow you. So the holy one to be born will be called the Son of God.

LUKE 1:35

JANUARY 21

To John, Jesus was a good friend with a good heart and a good idea.... Simple. To John, Jesus wasn't a treatise on social activism, nor was he a license for blowing up abortion clinics or living in a desert. Jesus was a friend.... Maybe that is why John is the only one of the twelve who was at the cross.... As far as he was concerned, his closest friend was in trouble and he came to help.

NO WONDER THEY CALL HIM THE SAVIOR, P. 88

I no longer call you servants.... Instead, I have called you friends.

JOHN 15:15

DECEMBER 11

An unseen Sculptor molds mud and dust.... A sudden breeze, surprisingly warm, whistles through the leaves scattering dust from the lifeless form. Winging on the warm wind is God's image. Laughter is laid in the sculpted cheeks. A reservoir of tears is stored in the soul. A sprinkling of twinkle for the eyes. Poetry for the spirit. Logic. Loyalty.... His Majesty smiles at his image. "It is good."

GOD CAME NEAR, P. 36

And the Lord God formed man from the dust of the ground and breathed into his nostrils the breath of life, and man became a living being.

GENESIS 2:7

JANUARY 22

Sense Jesus' power. Blind eyes...seeing. Fruitless tree...withering. Money changers...scampering. Religious leaders...cowering. Tomb...opening. Hear his promise. Death has no power. Failure holds no prisoners. Fear has no control. For God has come, God has come into your world...to take you home.

And the Angels Were Silent

Jesus called in a loud voice, "Lazarus, come out!" The dead man came out, his hands and feet wrapped with strips of linen, and a cloth around his face. Jesus said to them, "Take off the grave clothes and let him go."

John 11:43,44

DECEMBER 10

Jesus unmasked death and exposed him for who he really is—a ninety-eight-pound weakling dressed up in a Charles Atlas suit. Jesus had no patience for this impostor. He couldn't sit still while death pulled the veil over life.

SIX HOURS ONE FRIDAY, P. 134

I will ransom them from the power of the grave; I will redeem them from death.

HOSEA 13:14

JANUARY 23

Our values are messed up.... Thrills are going for top dollar and the value of human beings is at an all-time low.... Life is reduced to weekends, paychecks, and quick thrills. The bottom line is disaster.... Now please understand, this is man's value system. It is not God's. His plan is much brighter.

No Wonder They Call Him the Savior, pp. 33,34

Wisdom is supreme; therefore get wisdom. Though it cost all you have, get understanding.

Proverbs 4:7

DECEMBER 9

To know God is to receive his invitation. Not just to hear it, not just to study it, not just to acknowledge it, but to receive it. It is possible to learn much about God's invitation and never respond to it personally.

AND THE ANGELS WERE SILENT

Today, if you hear his voice, do not harden your hearts.

HEBREWS 4:7

JANUARY 24

A s Jesus stepped into the garden, you were in his prayers. As Jesus looked into heaven, you were in his vision. As Jesus dreamed of the day when we will be where he is, he saw you there. His final prayer was about you. His final pain was for you. His final passion was you.

AND THE ANGELS WERE SILENT

This is how we know what love is: Jesus Christ laid down his life for us.

1 JOHN 3:16

DECEMBER 8

The people stood watching, and the rulers even sneered at him. They said, "He saved others; let him save himself if he is the Christ of God, the Chosen One."

LUKE 23:35

The verbal stones were meant to sting. How Jesus, with a body wracked with pain, eyes blinded by his own blood, and lungs yearning for air, could speak on behalf of some heartless thugs is beyond my comprehension.... If ever a person deserved a shot at revenge, Jesus did.... Instead he died for them. How could he do it? I don't know. But I do know that all of a sudden my wounds seem very painless.

NO WONDER THEY CALL HIM THE SAVIOR, P. 25

JANUARY 25

God did what we wouldn't dare dream. He did what we couldn't imagine. He became a man so we could trust him. He became a sacrifice so we could know him. And he defeated death, so we could follow him.

AND THE ANGELS WERE SILENT

Since the children have flesh and blood, [Jesus] too shared in their humanity so that by his death he might destroy him who holds the power of death.

HEBREWS 2:14

DECEMBER 7

The saved may get close to the edge, they may even stumble and slide. But they will dig their nails into the rock of God and hang on.

AND THE ANGELS WERE SILENT

The LORD is my rock, my fortress and my deliverer; my God is my rock, in whom I take refuge, my shield and the horn of my salvation. He is my stronghold, my refuge and my savior.

2 SAMUEL 22:2,3

JANUARY 26

God as creator. Pensive. Excited. Inventive. An artist, brush on pallet, seeking the perfect shade. A composer, fingers on keyboard, listening for the exact chord. A poet, pen poised on paper, awaiting the precise word. The Creator, the master weaver, threading together the soul. Each one different. No two alike. None identical.

SIX HOURS ONE FRIDAY, PP. 92,93

The LORD God formed the man from the dust of the ground and breathed into his nostrils the breath of life.

GENESIS 2:7

DECEMBER 6

S eek the simple faith. Major in the majors. Focus on the critical. Long for God.

AND THE ANGELS WERE SILENT

Blessed are those who hunger and thirst for righteousness, for they will be filled.

MATTHEW 5:6

JANUARY 27

Jesus is the most active one at the table. Jesus is not portrayed as the one who reclines and receives, but the one who stands and gives. He still does. The Lord's Supper is a gift to you. The Lord's Supper is a sacrament, not a sacrifice.

AND THE ANGELS WERE SILENT

[Jesus] now showed [his disciples] the full extent of his love.... He got up from the meal, took off his outer clothing, and wrapped a towel around his waist. After that, he poured water into a basin and began to wash his disciples' feet, drying them with the towel that was wrapped around him.

JOHN 13:1,4,5

DECEMBER 5

Our problem is not so much that God doesn't give us what we hope for as it is that we don't know the right thing for which to hope. (You may want to read that sentence again.)

GOD CAME NEAR, P. 45

The Spirit helps us in our weakness. We do not know what we ought to pray for, but the Spirit himself intercedes for us with groans that words cannot express.

ROMANS 8:26

JANUARY 28

In becoming man, God made it possible for man to see God. When Jesus went home he left the back door open.

GOD CAME NEAR, P. 13

I am the way and the truth and the life. No one comes to the Father except through me.

JOHN 14:6

DECEMBER 4

God has a peculiar passion for the forgotten. Have you noticed? See his hand on the festered skin of the leper? See the face of the prostitute cupped in his hands? Notice how he responds to the touch of the woman with the hemorrhage? See him with his arm around little Zaccheus?

AND THE ANGELS WERE SILENT

Jesus said, "The Son of Man came to seek and to save what was lost."
LUKE 19:10

JANUARY 29

Jesus said, "Go to the village ahead of you, and at once you will find a donkey tied there, with her colt by her. Untie them and bring them to me. If anyone says anything to you, tell him that the Lord needs them, and he will send them right away."

MATTHEW 21:2,3

It could be that God wants to use your donkey to enter the walls of another city, another nation, another heart. Do you let him? Do you give it? Or do you hesitate? That guy who gave Jesus the donkey is just one in a long line of folks who gave little things to a big God.

AND THE ANGELS WERE SILENT

DECEMBER 3

Anchor points. Firm rocks sunk deeply in a solid foundation. Not casual opinions or negotiable hypotheses, but ironclad undeniables that will keep you afloat. How strong are yours? How sturdy is your life when faced with...storms?

SIX HOURS ONE FRIDAY, P. 16

No one can lay any foundation other than the one already laid, which is Jesus Christ.

1 CORINTHIANS 3:11

JANUARY 30

I'll say to myself, "You have plenty of good things laid up for many years. Take life easy; eat, drink and be merry." But God said to him, "You fool!"

LUKE 12:19,20

"One time won't hurt." "She'll never know." "Other people do much worse things." "At least you're not being hypocritical." Satan's rhetoric of rationalization never ends. The father of lies croons and woos like a traveling peddler, promising the moon and delivering disaster. "Step right up. Taste my brew of pleasure and sing my song of sensuality. After all, who knows about tomorrow?"

NO WONDER THEY CALL HIM THE SAVIOR, P. 81

DECEMBER 2

You created my inmost being; you knit me together in my mother's womb.

PSALM 139:13

"Knit together" is how the psalmist described the process of God making man. Not manufactured or mass-produced, but knitted. Each thread of personality tenderly intertwined. Each string of temperament deliberately selected.

SIX HOURS ONE FRIDAY, P. 92

JANUARY 31

Quit looking at life like an adult and see it through the eyes of a child. Essential counsel for us sober-minded, serious-faced, sour-pussed adults. Necessary advice for we Charles Atlas wannabes who shoulder the world. Good words for those of us who seldom say, "I can't wait until I wake up," and more often state, "I can't wait to go to bed."

AND THE ANGELS WERE SILENT

I tell you the truth, unless you change and become like little children, you will never enter the kingdom of heaven.

MATTHEW 18:3

DECEMBER 1

I t's the season to be jolly because, more than at any other time, we think of Jesus. More than in any other season, his name is on our lips.

GOD CAME NEAR, P. 22

Thou shalt call his name JESUS: for he shall save his people from their sins.

MATTHEW 1:21 KJV

FEBRUARY 1

ever were God's arms opened so wide as they were on the Roman cross. One arm extending back into history and the other reaching into the future. An embrace of forgiveness offered for anyone who'll come. A hen gathering her chicks. A father receiving his own. A redeemer redeeming the world. No wonder they call him the Savior.

NO WONDER THEY CALL HIM THE SAVIOR, P. 120

There is one God and one mediator between God and men, the man Christ Jesus, who gave himself as a ransom for all men.

1 TIMOTHY 2:5,6

NOVEMBER 30

Jesus said, "This gospel of the kingdom will be preached in the whole world as a testimony to all nations, and then the end will come."

MATTHEW 24:14

For those who live for this world, that's bad news. But for those who live for the world to come, it's an encouraging promise.

AND THE ANGELS WERE SILENT

FEBRUARY 2

Hungry bodies and cold hearts are easily found today. The counsel Jesus gives on surviving tough times is useful for more than the battles of Rome and Armageddon. It is useful for the battles of your world and mine.

AND THE ANGELS WERE SILENT

Therefore we do not lose heart. Though outwardly we are wasting away, yet inwardly we are being renewed day by day.

2 CORINTHIANS 4:16

NOVEMBER 29

The King of Kings will raise his pierced hand and proclaim, "No more." The angels will stand and the Father will speak, "No more." Every person who lives and who ever lived will turn toward the sky and hear God announce, "No more." No more loneliness. No more tears. No more death. No more sadness. No more crying. No more pain.

AND THE ANGELS WERE SILENT

I heard a loud voice from the throne saying, "Now the dwelling of God is with men, and he will live with them. They will be his people, and God himself will be with them."

REVELATION 21:3

FEBRUARY 3

H e's one of the underground's slyest agents—the agent of familiarity. His commission from the black throne room is clear and fatal: "Take nothing from your victim; cause him only to take everything for granted."... Hence, books will go unread, games will go unplayed, hearts will go unnurtured, and opportunities will go ignored. All because the poison of the ordinary has deadened your senses to the magic of the moment.

GOD CAME NEAR, PP. 74,75

Be very careful, then, how you live—not as unwise but as wise, making the most of every opportunity.

EPHESIANS 5:15,16

NOVEMBER 28

Jesus said, "Father, into your hands I commit my spirit."

LUKE 23:46

Were it a war—this would be the aftermath. Were it a symphony—this would be the second between the final note and the first applause. Were it a journey—this would be the sight of home. Were it a storm—this would be the sun, piercing the clouds. But it wasn't. It was a Messiah. And this was a sigh of joy.

NO WONDER THEY CALL HIM THE SAVIOR, P. 65

FEBRUARY 4

I dare say that all of us have witnessed our sandcastle promises swept away by the pounding waves of panic and insecurity. I imagine that all of us have seen our words of promise and obedience ripped into ribbons by the chainsaw of fear and fright. And I haven't met a person yet who hasn't done the very thing he swore he would never do.

NO WONDER THEY CALL HIM THE SAVIOR, P. 85

Peter declared, "Even if all fall away, I will not."

MARK 14:29

NOVEMBER 27

We think God's love rises and falls with our performance. It doesn't.... He loves you for whose you are: you are his child.

AND THE ANGELS WERE SILENT

To all who received him, to those who believed in his name, he gave the right to become children of God.

JOHN 1:12

FEBRUARY 5

Sure you can have a second chance. Just ask Peter. One minute he felt lower than a snake's belly and the next minute he was the high hog at the trough. Even the angels wanted this distraught netcaster to know that it wasn't over. The message came loud and clear from the celestial Throne Room through the divine courier. "Be sure and tell Peter that he gets to bat again."

No Wonder They Call Him the Savior, pp. 94,95

"Don't be alarmed," he said.... "He has risen! ...Go tell his disciples and Peter."

Mark 16:6,7

NOVEMBER 26

Man was not created to be separated from his creator; hence he sighs, longing for home. The creation was never intended to be inhabited by evil; hence she sighs, yearning for the Garden. And the conversations with God were never intended to depend on a translator; hence the Spirit groans on our behalf, looking to a day when humans will see God face to face.

GOD CAME NEAR, P. 31

Now we see but a poor reflection as in a mirror; then we shall see face to face.

1 CORINTHIANS 13:12

FEBRUARY 6

A repentant heart is all he demands. Come out of the shadows! Be done with your hiding! A repentant heart is enough to summon the Son of God himself to walk through our walls of guilt and shame. He who forgave Peter stands ready to forgive the rest of us. All we have to do is come back. No wonder they call him the Savior.

NO WONDER THEY CALL HIM THE SAVIOR, P. 86

When the disciples were together, with the doors locked for fear of the Jews, Jesus came and stood among them and said, "Peace be with you!"

JOHN 20:19

NOVEMBER 25

God wants you to fly. He wants you to fly free of yesterday's guilt. He wants you to fly free of today's fears. He wants you to fly free of tomorrow's grave. Sin, fear, and death. These are the mountains he has moved. These are the prayers he will answer. That is the fruit he will grant. This is what he longs to do: he longs to set you free so you can fly...fly home.

AND THE ANGELS WERE SILENT

Those who hope in the LORD will renew their strength. They will soar on wings like eagles.

ISAIAH 40:31

FEBRUARY 7

A mbition is that grit in the soul which creates disenchantment with the ordinary and puts the dare into dreams.

GOD CAME NEAR, P. 60

Do you see a man skilled in his work? He will serve before kings; he will not serve before obscure men.

PROVERBS 22:29

NOVEMBER 24

God's invitation is not just for a meal...it is for life. An invitation to come into his kingdom and take up residence in a tearless, graveless, painless world. Who can come? Whoever wishes. The invitation is at once universal and personal.

AND THE ANGELS WERE SILENT

God himself will be with them and be their God. There will be no more **death** or mourning or crying or pain.

REVELATION 21:3,4

GOD CAME NEAR

FEBRUARY 8

The centurion sat on a rock and stared at the three silhouetted figures. Their heads were limp, occasionally rolling from side to side.... Suddenly the center head...yanked itself erect.... A roar silenced the silence. "It is finished." It wasn't a yell. It wasn't a scream. It was a roar, a lion's roar. From what world that roar came the centurion didn't know, but he knew it wasn't this one.

SIX HOURS ONE FRIDAY, P. 234

When the centurion, who stood there in front of Jesus, heard his cry and saw how he died, he said, "Surely this man was the Son of God!"

MARK 15:39

NOVEMBER 23

God is a God who invites. God is a God who calls. God is a God who opens the door and waves his hand pointing pilgrims to a full table.

AND THE ANGELS WERE SILENT

Come, all you who are thirsty, come to the waters; and you who have no money, come, buy and eat! Come, buy wine and milk without money and without cost.

ISAIAH 55:1

FEBRUARY 9

Silently the Divine Surgeon reached into his kit and pulled out a needle of faith and a thread of hope. In the shade of Jacob's well he stitched her wounded soul back together. "There will come a day..." he whispered.

GOD CAME NEAR, P. 28

Jesus answered [the Samaritan woman], "If you knew the gift of God and who it is that asks you for a drink, you would have asked him and he would have given you living water."

JOHN 4:10

NOVEMBER 22

Christianity, in its purest form, is nothing more than seeing Jesus. Christian service, in its purest form, is nothing more than imitating him whom we see. To see His Majesty and to imitate him, that is the sum of Christianity.

GOD CAME NEAR, P. 6

Be imitators of God, therefore, as dearly loved children.

EPHESIANS 5:1

FEBRUARY 10

A woman was there who had been subject to bleeding for twelve years. She had...spent all she had.... She came up behind [Jesus] in the crowd and touched his cloak.

MARK 5:25-27

It didn't bother Jesus that the woman came to him as a last resort. To him it mattered only that she came. He knows that with some of us it takes a lot of reality to snap us to our senses, so he doesn't keep a time clock. Those who scramble in at quitting time get the same wage as those who beat the morning whistle. I guess that's what makes grace, grace.

GOD CAME NEAR, P. 28

NOVEMBER 21

John is the only one of the twelve who was at the cross.... His closest friend was in trouble and he came to help. "Can you take care of my mother?" Of course. That's what friends are for. John teaches us that the strongest relationship with Christ may not necessarily be a complicated one.

NO WONDER THEY CALL HIM THE SAVIOR, P. 88

I have called you friends, for everything that I learned from my Father I have made known to you.

JOHN 15:15

FEBRUARY 11

How your heart must have ached as you heard the cracking voice of your son, "Father, take this cup away." You released Jesus into a hostile arena with a cruel soldier who turned the back of your son into raw meat.... You said good-bye to Jesus knowing he would be spat upon, laughed at, and killed.

SIX HOURS ONE FRIDAY, P. 51

He was pierced for our transgressions, he was crushed for our iniquities; the punishment that brought us peace was upon him, and by his wounds we are healed.

ISAIAH 53:5

NOVEMBER 20

Defining Jesus would be a challenge to the best of writers, but John handles the task with casual analogy. The Messiah, in a word, was "the Word." A walking message. A love letter. Be he a fiery verb or a tender adjective, he was, quite simply, a word.

NO WONDER THEY CALL HIM THE SAVIOR, P. 87

In the beginning was the Word, and the Word was with God, and the Word was God.

JOHN 1:1

FEBRUARY 12

You, God, said good-bye to your son fully aware that when he would need you the most, when his cry of despair would roar through the heavens, you would sit in silence. The angels, though positioned, would hear no command from you. Your son, though in anguish, would feel no comfort from your hands. "He gave his best," the Apostle Paul reasons, "why should we doubt his love?"

SIX HOURS ONE FRIDAY, P. 52

He that spared not his own Son, but delivered him up for us all, how shall he not with him also freely give us all things?

ROMANS 8:32 KJV

NOVEMBER 19

Could you do it all over again, you'd do it differently. You'd be a different person. You'd be more patient. You'd control your tongue. You'd finish what you started. You'd turn the other cheek instead of slapping his. You'd get married first. You wouldn't marry at all. You'd be honest. You'd resist the temptation. You'd run with a different crowd. But you can't.

SIX HOURS ONE FRIDAY, P. 199

Don't act thoughtlessly, but try to find out and do whatever the Lord wants you to.

EPHESIANS 5:17 TLB

FEBRUARY 13

P ilate almost performed what would have been history's greatest act of mercy. He almost pardoned the Prince of Peace. He almost released the Son of God. He almost opted to acquit the Christ. Almost. He had the power. He had the choice. He wore the signet ring. The option to free God's Son was his...and he did it...almost.

NO WONDER THEY CALL HIM THE SAVIOR, P. 80

Do not withhold good from those who deserve it, when it is in your power to act.

PROVERBS 3:27

NOVEMBER 18

Over and over again God wants us to get the message: He has a peculiar passion for the forgotten. What society puts out, God puts in. What the world writes off, God picks up.

AND THE ANGELS WERE SILENT

Jesus said, "I am the good shepherd. The good shepherd lays down his life for the sheep."

JOHN 10:11

FEBRUARY 14

I t defies logic. It is a divine insanity. A holy incredibility. Only a God beyond systems and common sense could create a plan as absurd as this. Yet, it is the very impossibility of it all that makes it possible. The wildness of the story is its strongest witness. For only a God could create a plan this mad. Only a creator beyond the fence of logic could offer such a gift of love.

AND THE ANGELS WERE SILENT

For God so loved the world that he gave his one and only Son, that whoever believes in him shall not perish but have eternal life.

JOHN 3:16

NOVEMBER 17

The one to whom we pray knows our feelings. He knows temptation. He has felt discouraged. He has been hungry and sleepy and tired. He knows what we feel like when the alarm clock goes off.... He is touched when we tell him there is more to do than can ever be done.... "I'm thirsty." That's not THE CHRIST that's thirsty. That's the carpenter. And those are words of humanity in the midst of divinity.

NO WONDER THEY CALL HIM THE SAVIOR, PP. 52,53

Jesus said, "I am thirsty."

JOHN 19:28

FEBRUARY 15

God will do what it takes—whatever it takes—to bring his children home.

AND THE ANGELS WERE SILENT

This is how God showed his love among us: He sent his one and only Son into the world that we might live through him.

1 JOHN 4:9

NOVEMBER 16

To love conditionally is against God's nature. Just as it's against your nature to eat trees and against mine to grow wings, it's against God's nature to remember forgiven sins.

GOD CAME NEAR, P. 51

I will forgive their wickedness and will remember their sins no more.
HEBREWS 8:12

GOD
CAME NEAR

FEBRUARY 16

Jesus was human. He wants us to know that he, too, knew the drone of the humdrum and the weariness that comes with long days. He wants us to remember that our trailblazer didn't wear bulletproof vests or rubber gloves or an impenetrable suit of armor. No, he pioneered our salvation through the world that you and I face daily.

NO WONDER THEY CALL HIM THE SAVIOR, P. 53

Looking unto Jesus the author and finisher of our faith.

HEBREWS 12:2 KJV

NOVEMBER 15

D on't we all long for a father who, even though our mistakes are written all over the wall, will love us anyway? Don't we want a father who cares for us in spite of our failures? We do have that type of a father. A father who is at his best when we are at our worst. A father whose grace is strongest when our devotion is weakest.

SIX HOURS ONE FRIDAY, P. 85

This, then, is how you should pray: "Our Father in heaven...."

MATTHEW 6:9

FEBRUARY 17

S ometimes I wonder if we don't see Christ's love as much in the people he tolerated as in the pain he endured. Amazing Grace.

NO WONDER THEY CALL HIM THE SAVIOR, P. 26

Again and again they struck him on the head with a staff and spit on him.

MARK 15:19

NOVEMBER 14

A re you close to quitting? Please don't do it. Are you discouraged as a parent? Hang in there. Are you weary with doing good? Do just a little more. Are you pessimistic about your job? Roll up your sleeves and go at it again. No communication in your marriage? Give it one more shot.... Is hope a forgotten word?... The Land of Promise, says Jesus, awaits those who endure.

NO WONDER THEY CALL HIM THE SAVIOR, P. 62

If we endure, we will also reign with him.

2 TIMOTHY 2:12

FEBRUARY 18

I t's a sad but true fact of the faith: religion is used for profit and prestige. And when it is, there are two results: people are exploited and God is infuriated.

AND THE ANGELS WERE SILENT

Religion that God our Father accepts as pure and faultless is this: to look after orphans and widows in their distress and to keep oneself from being polluted by the world.

JAMES 1:27

NOVEMBER 13

R e-liable. Liable means responsible. Re means over and over again.

GOD CAME NEAR, P. 67

Let us not become weary in doing good, for at the proper time we will reap a harvest if we do not give up.

GALATIANS 6:9

FEBRUARY 19

There are some who position themselves between you and God. There are some who suggest that the only way to get to God is through them.... Jesus' message for complicated religion is to remove these middlemen.... We are all brothers and sisters and have equal access to the Father.

AND THE ANGELS WERE SILENT

You are not to be called "Rabbi," for you have only one Master and you are all brothers.

MATTHEW 23:8

NOVEMBER 12

If you ever want to know how to conduct yourself at a funeral, don't look to Jesus for an example. He interrupted each one he ever attended. A lifeguard can't sit still while someone is drowning. A teacher can't resist helping when a student is confused. And Jesus couldn't watch a funeral and do nothing.

SIX HOURS ONE FRIDAY, P. 134

For the Lord himself will come down from heaven, with a loud command, with the voice of the archangel and with the trumpet call of God, and the dead in Christ will rise.

1 THESSALONIANS 4:16

FEBRUARY 20

A s much out of desperation as inspiration, Martha said yes. As she studied the tan face of that Galilean carpenter, something told her she'd probably never get closer to the truth than she was right now.

GOD CAME NEAR, P. 34

Jesus said to [Martha], "I am the resurrection and the life. He who believes in me will live, even though he dies; and whoever lives and believes in me will never die. Do you believe this?" "Yes, Lord," she told him.

JOHN 11:25-27

NOVEMBER 11

W e were born out of one eternity and are frighteningly close to another. We play tag with the fuzzy realities of death and pain. We can't answer our own questions about love and hurt. We can't solve the riddle of aging. We can't keep ourselves out of war. We can't even keep ourselves fed. Paul spoke for humanity when he confessed, "I do not know what I am doing" (Romans 7:15, author's paraphrase).

No Wonder They Call Him the Savior, pp. 29,30

The foolishness of God is wiser than man's wisdom, and the weakness of God is stronger than man's strength.

1 Corinthians 1:25

FEBRUARY 21

It is a hinge point in history. A chink has been found in death's armor. The keys to the halls of hell have been claimed.... Life confronts death—and wins! The wind stops. A cloud blocks the sun and a bird chirps in the distance while a humiliated snake slithers between the rocks and disappears into the ground. The stage has been set for a confrontation at Calvary.

GOD CAME NEAR, P. 33

Jesus called in a loud voice, "Lazarus, come out!"

JOHN 11:43

NOVEMBER 10

Loneliness. It's a cry, a moan, a wail. It's a gasp whose origin is the recesses of our souls. Can you hear it? The abandoned child. The divorcee. The quiet home. The empty mailbox. The long days. The longer nights. A one-night stand. A forgotten birthday. A silent phone.

NO WONDER THEY CALL HIM THE SAVIOR, P. 45

If I rise on the wings of the dawn, if I settle on the far side of the sea, even there your hand will guide me, your right hand will hold me fast.

PSALM 139:9,10

FEBRUARY 22

D o you show contempt for the riches of his kindness, tolerance and patience, not realizing that God's kindness leads you toward repentance?

ROMANS 2:4

The purpose of God's patience? Our repentance.

AND THE ANGELS WERE SILENT

NOVEMBER 9

The people came. They came out of the cul-de-sacs and office complexes of their day. They brought Jesus the burdens of their existence and he gave them not religion, not doctrine, not systems, but rest. As a result, they called him Lord. As a result, they called him Savior.

SIX HOURS ONE FRIDAY, PP. 32,33

Jesus said, "Come to me, all you who are weary and burdened, and I will give you rest."

MATTHEW 11:28

FEBRUARY 23

God is patient with our mistakes. He is longsuffering with our stumbles. He doesn't get angry at our questions. He doesn't turn away when we struggle. But when we repeatedly reject his message, when we are insensitive to his pleadings, when he changes history itself to get our attention and we still don't listen, he honors our request.

AND THE ANGELS WERE SILENT

A man who remains stiff-necked after many rebukes will suddenly be destroyed—without remedy.

PROVERBS 29:1

NOVEMBER 8

W hat kind of God would give you families and then ask you to leave them? What kind of God would give you friends and then ask you to say goodbye? A God who knows that the deepest love is built not on passion and romance but on a common mission and sacrifice. A God who knows that we are only pilgrims and that eternity is so close that any "Goodbye" is in reality a "See you tomorrow." A God who did it himself.

No Wonder They Call Him the Savior, p. 41

[He] made himself nothing, taking the very nature of a servant, being made in human likeness.

Philippians 2:7

FEBRUARY 24

In astounding tandem a human body housed divinity. Holiness and earthliness intertwined.

GOD CAME NEAR, P. 7

But when the fulness of the time was come, God sent forth his Son, made of a woman, made under law.

GALATIANS 4:4 KJV

NOVEMBER 7

Religion is the hoax Jesus is out to disclose.... The faith is not in religion, the faith is in God. A hardy, daring faith which believes God will do what is right, every time. And that God will do what it takes—whatever it takes—to bring his children home.

AND THE ANGELS WERE SILENT

I am the gate for the sheep. All who ever came before me were thieves and robbers, but the sheep did not listen to them. The thief comes only to steal and kill and destroy; I have come that they may have life, and have it to the full.

JOHN 10:7,8,10

FEBRUARY 25

J esus lives in the forgotten. He has taken up residence in the ignored. He has made a mansion amidst the ill. If we want to see God we must go among the broken and beaten and there we will see him.

AND THE ANGELS WERE SILENT

Inasmuch as ye have done it unto one of the least of these my brethren, ye have done it unto me.

MATTHEW 25:40 KJV

NOVEMBER 6

Quit looking at life like an adult and see it through the eyes of a child.

AND THE ANGELS WERE SILENT

I tell you the truth, anyone who will not receive the kingdom of God like a little child will never enter it.

MARK 10:15

FEBRUARY 26

Jesus' death was not the result of a panicking, cosmological engineer. The cross wasn't a tragic surprise. Calvary was not a knee-jerk response to a world plummeting towards destruction. It wasn't a patch-job or a stop-gap measure. The death of the Son of God was anything but an unexpected peril. No, it was part of a plan. It was a calculated choice.

GOD CAME NEAR, P. 39

[Jesus] was handed over...by God's set purpose and foreknowledge.

ACTS 2:23

NOVEMBER 5

Jesus. Have you seen him? Those who first did were never the same.

GOD CAME NEAR, P. 7

These...have turned the world upside down.

ACTS 17:6 KJV

FEBRUARY 27

The divinity of Christ assured the humanity of Christ, and Jesus spoke loud enough for the pits of hell to vibrate: "On the third day he will be raised to life."

AND THE ANGELS WERE SILENT

The Son of Man is going to be betrayed into the hands of men. They will kill him, and on the third day he will be raised to life.

MATTHEW 17:22,23

NOVEMBER 4

The dead man sat up and began to talk, and Jesus gave him back to his mother.

LUKE 7:15

Jesus gave the woman much more than her son. He gave her a secret—a whisper that was overheard by us. "That," he said pointing at the cot, "that is fantasy. This," he grinned, putting an arm around the boy, "this is reality."

SIX HOURS ONE FRIDAY, P. 222

FEBRUARY 28

Word has it that the Creator's tireless hands are preparing a city so glorious that even the angels get goosebumps upon seeing it. Considering what he has done so far, that is one creation I plan to see.

NO WONDER THEY CALL HIM THE SAVIOR, P. 58

In my Father's house are many rooms; if it were not so, I would have told you. I am going there to prepare a place for you.

JOHN 14:2

NOVEMBER 3

A s [Jesus] approached the town gate, a dead person was being carried out—the only son of his mother,...a widow. When the Lord saw her, his heart went out to her and he said, "Don't cry."

LUKE 7:12,13

How would you feel at a moment like this? What would you do? A stranger tells you not to weep as you look at your dead son. One who refused to mourn in the midst of sorrow calls the devil's bluff, then shocks you with a call into the cavern of death. Suddenly what had been taken is returned. What had been stolen is retrieved. What you had given up, you are given back.

SIX HOURS ONE FRIDAY, P. 221

FEBRUARY 29

There was a time when if [Jesus] could have, he would have turned his back on the whole mess and gone away. But he couldn't. He couldn't because he saw you. He saw you betrayed by those you love. He saw you with a body which gets sick and a heart which grows weak. He saw you in your own garden of gnarled trees and sleeping friends. He saw you staring into the pit of your own failures and the mouth of your own grave.

AND THE ANGELS WERE SILENT

The Son of Man did not come to be served, but to serve, and to give his life as a ransom for many.

MARK 10:45

NOVEMBER 2

The most gut-wrenching cry of loneliness in history came not from a prisoner or a widow or a patient. It came from a hill, from a cross, from a Messiah.... Never have words carried so much hurt. Never has one being been so lonely.

NO WONDER THEY CALL HIM THE SAVIOR, P. 47

Jesus cried out in a loud voice..."My God, my God, why have you forsaken me?"

MARK 15:34

MARCH 1

Two trees. One is weathered and leafless. It is dead but still sturdy.... Only bare branches fork from the trunk. On the strongest of these branches is tied a hangman's noose. It was here that Judas dealt with his failure. If only Judas had looked at the adjacent tree. It is also dead; its wood is also smooth. But there is no noose tied to its crossbeam. No more death on this tree. Once was enough. One death for all.

NO WONDER THEY CALL HIM THE SAVIOR, P. 90

For Christ's love compels us, because we are convinced that one died for all, and therefore all died.

2 CORINTHIANS 5:14

NOVEMBER 1

Simplify your faith by seeking God for yourself.... You got a Bible? You can study. You got a heart? You can pray. You got a mind? You can think.

AND THE ANGELS WERE SILENT, P. 15:78

Seek the Lord while he may be found; call on him while he is near.

ISAIAH 55:6

MARCH 2

To say there is no hell is to portray God with eyes blind to the hunger and evil in the world. To say there is no hell is to say that God doesn't care that people are beaten and massacred, that he doesn't care that women are raped or families wrecked. To say there is no hell is to say God has no justice, no sense of right and wrong, and eventually to say God has no love. For true love hates what is evil.

AND THE ANGELS WERE SILENT

The LORD...will not leave the guilty unpunished.

NAHUM 1:3

OCTOBER 31

E ven after generations of people had spit in his face, he still loved them.... And yet, it is that very irrationality that gives the gospel its greatest defense. For only God could love like that.

GOD CAME NEAR, P. 16

They all condemned him as worthy of death. Then some began to spit at him.

MARK 14:64,65

MARCH 3

ell is the chosen place of the person who loves self more than God, who loves sin more than his Savior, who loves this world more than God's world. Judgment is that moment when God looks at the rebellious and says, "Your choice will be honored."

AND THE ANGELS WERE SILENT

Rend your heart and not your garments. Return to the LORD your God, for he is gracious and compassionate, slow to anger and abounding in love, and he relents from sending calamity.

JOEL 2:13

OCTOBER 30

The way to handle a person's behavior is to understand the cause of it. One way to deal with a person's peculiarities is to try to understand why they are peculiar.

AND THE ANGELS WERE SILENT

Do to others as you would have them do to you.

LUKE 6:31

MARCH 4

I t's the great triumph of heaven: God is on the earth. And it is the great tragedy of earth: man has rejected God.

AND THE ANGELS WERE SILENT

He came to that which was his own, but his own did not receive him.

JOHN 1:11

OCTOBER 29

As the echo of the crunching of apple was still sounding in the garden [of Eden], Jesus was leaving for Calvary.

AND THE ANGELS WERE SILENT

...the Lamb that was slain from the creation of the world.

REVELATION 13:8

MARCH 5

J esus called himself divine, yet allowed a minimum-wage Roman
soldier to drive a nail into his wrist. He demanded purity, yet stood
for the rights of a repentant whore.

GOD CAME NEAR, P. 7

Who is a God like you, who pardons sin and forgives...transgression?

MICAH 7:18

OCTOBER 28

Man by himself cannot deal with his own guilt. He must have help from the outside. In order to forgive himself, he must have forgiveness from the one he has offended. Yet man is unworthy to ask God for forgiveness. That, then, is the whole reason for the cross.

No Wonder They Call Him the Savior, pp. 139,140

When I kept silent, my bones wasted away through my groaning all day long.... Then I acknowledged my sin to you.... And you forgave the guilt of my sin.

Psalm 32:3,5

GOD CAME NEAR

MARCH 6

He called men to march, yet refused to allow them to call him King. He sent men into all the world, yet equipped them with only bended knees and memories of a resurrected carpenter.

GOD CAME NEAR, P. 7

Peace be with you! As the Father has sent me, I am sending you.

JOHN 20:21

OCTOBER 27

Before you know it, the little face that brought tears to your eyes in the delivery room can become—perish the thought—common. A common kid sitting in the back seat of your van as you whiz down the fast lane of life. Unless something changes, unless someone wakes you up, that common kid will become a common stranger.

GOD CAME NEAR, P. 75

Sons are a heritage from the LORD, children a reward from him.

PSALM 127:3

MARCH 7

If you've always thought of Jesus as a pale-faced, milque-toast-Tiny Tim, then read Matthew 23 and see the other side: an angry father denouncing the pimps who have prostituted his children. Six times he calls them hypocrites. Five times he calls them blind. Seven times he denounces them and once he prophecies their ruin.

AND THE ANGELS WERE SILENT

Jesus said, "Woe to you, teachers of the law and Pharisees, you hypocrites! You have neglected the more important matters of the law—justice, mercy and faithfulness."

MATTHEW 23:23

OCTOBER 26

If there is a scene in this story that deserves to be framed, it's the one of the father's outstretched hands. His tears are moving. His smile is stirring. But his hands call us home. Imagine those hands. Strong fingers. Palms wrinkled with lifelines. Stretching open like a wide gate, leaving entrance as the only option.

SIX HOURS ONE FRIDAY, PP. 114,115

He ran to his son, threw his arms around him and kissed him.

LUKE 15:20

MARCH 8

Just trying to picture the scene is enough to short-circuit the most fanciful of imaginations; a flatnosed ex-con asking God's son for eternal life? But trying to imagine the appeal being honored, well, that steps beyond the realm of reality and enters absurdity. But as absurd as it may appear, that's exactly what happened. He who deserved hell got heaven.

NO WONDER THEY CALL HIM THE SAVIOR, P. 31

Jesus answered him, "I tell you the truth, today you will be with me in paradise."

LUKE 23:43

OCTOBER 25

The son had no money. He had no excuses. And he had no idea how much his father had missed him.... The boy had no idea the number of times his father had awakened from restless sleep, gone into the boy's room, and sat on his bed. And the son would never have believed the hours the father had sat on the porch next to the empty rocking chair, looking, longing to see that familiar figure, that stride, that face.

SIX HOURS ONE FRIDAY, P. 113

[The son] got up and went to his father. But while he was still a long way off, his father saw him and was filled with compassion for him.

LUKE 15:20

MARCH 9

Forget any suggestion that Jesus was trapped. Erase any theory that Jesus made a miscalculation. Ignore any speculation that the cross was a last-ditch attempt to salvage a dying mission. For if these words tell us anything, they tell us that Jesus died...on purpose. No surprise. No hesitation. No faltering.

AND THE ANGELS WERE SILENT

Jesus said, "We are going up to Jerusalem, and the Son of Man will be betrayed to the chief priests and the teachers of the law. They will condemn him to death and will turn him over to the Gentiles to be mocked and flogged and crucified."

MATTHEW 20:18,19

OCTOBER 24

In the agony of Jesus lies our hope. Had he not sighed, had he not felt the burden for what was not intended, we would be in a pitiful condition.... That holy sigh assures us that God still groans for his people. He groans for the day when all sighs will cease, when what was intended to be will be.

GOD CAME NEAR, P. 31

Therefore he is able to save completely those who come to God through him, because he always lives to intercede for them.

HEBREWS 7:25

MARCH 10

Hopelessly stranded on death row, Barabbas wasn't about to balk at a granted stay of execution. Maybe he didn't understand mercy and surely he didn't deserve it, but he wasn't about to refuse it. We might do well to realize that our plight isn't too different than that of Barabbas. We, too, are prisoners with no chance for appeal. But why some prefer to stay in prison while the cell door has been unlocked is a mystery worth pondering.

NO WONDER THEY CALL HIM THE SAVIOR, PP. 76,77

It is for freedom that Christ has set us free. Stand firm, then.

GALATIANS 5:1

OCTOBER 23

No angelic shield protected his back from the whip. No holy helmet shielded his brow from the thorny crown. God crawled neck deep into the mire of humanity, plunged into the darkest cave of death, and emerged—alive.

AND THE ANGELS WERE SILENT

Then Pilate took Jesus and had him flogged. The soldiers twisted **together** a crown of thorns and put it on his head.

JOHN 19:1,2

MARCH 11

S kull's hill—windswept and stony. The thief—gaunt and pale....
He's taking the last step down the spiral staircase of failure.... He
sees Jesus.... He hears the hoarse whisper, "Father, forgive them."
He sees the sign above Jesus' head. It's painted with sarcasm: King of
the Jews.... If he were crazy, they would ignore him.... You only kill a
king if he has a kingdom. Could it be?

SIX HOURS ONE FRIDAY, PP. 124,125

Pilate had a notice...fastened to the cross. It read: Jesus of Nazareth, the
King of the Jews.

JOHN 19:19

OCTOBER 22

P ilate has an opportunity to perform the world's greatest act of mercy—and he doesn't. God is in his house and Pilate doesn't see him.

AND THE ANGELS WERE SILENT

Finally Pilate handed him over to them to be crucified.

JOHN 19:16

MARCH 12

The other criminal rebuked him. "Don't you fear God," he said, "since you are under the same sentence? We are punished justly, for we are getting what our deeds deserve. But this man has done nothing wrong."

LUKE 23:40,41

Lodged in the thief's statement are the two facts that anyone needs to recognize in order to come to Jesus.... "We are getting what our deeds deserve. But this man has done nothing wrong." We are guilty and he is innocent. We are filthy and he is pure. We are wrong and he is right. He is not on that cross for his sins. He is there for ours.

SIX HOURS ONE FRIDAY, P. 127

OCTOBER 21

J esus said, "Father, forgive them, for they do not know what they are doing."

LUKE 23:34

Words of chance muttered by a desperate martyr? No. Words of intent, painted by the Divine Deliverer on the canvas of sacrifice.

NO WONDER THEY CALL HIM THE SAVIOR, P. 21

MARCH 13

No stained-glass homilies. No excuses. Just a desperate plea for help. At this point Jesus performs the greatest miracle of the cross. Greater than the earthquake. Greater than the tearing of the temple curtain. Greater than the darkness. Greater than the resurrected saints appearing on the streets. He performs the miracle of forgiveness.

SIX HOURS ONE FRIDAY, P. 127

Jesus, remember me when you come into your kingdom.

LUKE 23:42

OCTOBER 20

One glimpse of the King and you are consumed by a desire to see more of him and say more about him. Pew-warming is no longer an option. Junk religion will no longer suffice. Sensation-seeking is needless. Once you have seen his face you will forever long to see it again.

GOD CAME NEAR, P. 7

We would see Jesus.

JOHN 12:21 KJV

MARCH 14

Wow. Only seconds before, the thief was a beggar nervously squeezing his hat at the castle door, wondering if the King might spare a few crumbs. Suddenly he's holding the whole pantry. Such is the definition of grace.

SIX HOURS ONE FRIDAY, P. 128

I tell you the truth, today you will be with me in paradise.

LUKE 23:43

OCTOBER 19

All of us have a donkey. You and I each have something in our lives, which, if given back to God, could, like the donkey, move Jesus and his story further down the road. Maybe you can sing or hug or program a computer or speak Swahili or write a check. Whichever, that's your donkey. Whichever, your donkey belongs to him.

AND THE ANGELS WERE SILENT

Jesus said, "Go to the village ahead of you, and at once you will find a donkey tied there, with her colt by her. Untie them and bring them to me."

MATTHEW 21:2

MARCH 15

Something about the crucifixion made every witness either step toward it or away from it. And today, two thousand years later, the same is true. It's the watershed. It's the Continental Divide. And you are either on one side or the other. A choice is demanded.... No fence sitting is permitted.... That is one luxury that God, in his awful mercy, doesn't permit. On which side are you?

NO WONDER THEY CALL HIM THE SAVIOR, P. 73

I tell you the truth, unless you eat the flesh of the Son of Man and drink his blood, you have no life in you.

JOHN 6:53

OCTOBER 18

W e, like Thomas, find it hard to believe that God can do the very thing that he is best at; replacing death with life. Our infertile imaginations bear little hope that the improbable will occur. We then, like Thomas, let our dreams fall victim to doubt. We make the same mistake that Thomas made: we forget that "impossible" is one of God's favorite words.

NO WONDER THEY CALL HIM THE SAVIOR, P. 99

[Thomas] said to them, "Unless I see the nail marks in his hands and put my finger where the nails were, and put my hand into his side, I will not believe it."

JOHN 20:25

MARCH 16

Jesus was born crucified. Whenever he became conscious of who he was, he also became conscious of what he had to do. The cross-shaped shadow could always be seen. And the screams of hell's imprisoned could always be heard.

GOD CAME NEAR, P. 39

...the Lamb slain from the foundation of the world.

REVELATION 13:8 KJV

OCTOBER 17

The right heart with the wrong ritual is better than the wrong heart with the right ritual.

AND THE ANGELS WERE SILENT

Many people...had not purified themselves, yet they ate the Passover, contrary to what was written. But Hezekiah prayed for them, saying, "May the LORD, who is good, pardon everyone who sets his heart on seeking God...even if he is not clean according to the rules of the sanctuary." And the LORD heard Hezekiah and healed the people.

2 CHRONICLES 30:18-20

MARCH 17

I t's an inexplicable dilemma—how two people can hear the same words and see the same Savior, and one see hope and the other see nothing but himself.

SIX HOURS ONE FRIDAY, P. 215

One of the criminals who hung there hurled insults at him: "Aren't you the Christ? Save yourself and us!" But the other criminal rebuked him.

LUKE 23:39,40

OCTOBER 16

Hope is not what you expect; it is what you would never dream. It is a wild, improbable tale with a pinch-me-I'm-dreaming ending. It's Abraham adjusting his bifocals so he can see not his grandson, but his son. It's Moses standing in the promised land not with Aaron or Miriam at his side, but with Elijah and the transfigured Christ.

GOD CAME NEAR, P. 45

Hope that is seen is no hope at all. Who hopes for what he already has?
ROMANS 8:24

MARCH 18

Y ou can't forgive me for my sins nor can I forgive you for yours. Two kids in a mud puddle can't clean each other. They need someone clean. Someone spotless. We need someone clean too. That's why we need a savior.

NO WONDER THEY CALL HIM THE SAVIOR, P. 140

We do not have a high priest who is unable to sympathize with our weaknesses, but we have one who has been tempted in every way, just as we are—yet was without sin.

HEBREWS 4:15

OCTOBER 15

Remember Jesus. Remember holiness in tandem with humanity. Remember the sick who were healed with calloused hands. Remember the dead called from the grave with a Galilean accent. Remember the eyes of God that wept human tears. And, most of all, remember this descendant of David who defeated death.

SIX HOURS ONE FRIDAY, P. 76

Where, O death, is your victory? Where, O death, is your sting?

1 CORINTHIANS 15:55

MARCH 19

Jesus looked around the carpentry shop. He stood for a moment in the refuge of the little room that housed so many sweet memories.... Among the voices that found their way into that carpentry shop in Nazareth was your voice. Your silent prayers uttered on tear-stained pillows were heard before they were said. Your deepest questions about death and eternity were answered before they were asked.

GOD CAME NEAR, PP. 24,25

Let us then approach the throne of grace with confidence, so that we may receive mercy and find grace to help us in our time of need.

HEBREWS 4:16

OCTOBER 14

When times get hard, remember Jesus. When people don't listen, remember Jesus. When tears come, remember Jesus. When disappointment is your bedpartner, remember Jesus. When fear pitches his tent in your front yard. When death looms, when anger singes, when shame weighs heavily. Remember Jesus.

SIX HOURS ONE FRIDAY, P. 76

Remember Jesus Christ, raised from the dead, descended from David.

2 TIMOTHY 2:8

MARCH 20

Jesus left the carpentry shop because of you. He laid his security down with his hammer. He hung tranquility on the peg with his nail apron. He closed the window shutters on the sunshine of his youth and locked the door on the comfort and ease of anonymity. Since he could bear your sins more easily than he could bear the thought of your hopelessness, he chose to leave.

GOD CAME NEAR, P. 25

Christ in you, the hope of glory.

COLOSSIANS 1:27

OCTOBER 13

Never did the obscene come so close to the holy as it did on Calvary. Never did the good in the world so tightly intertwine with the bad as it did on the cross. Never did what is right involve itself so intimately with what is wrong, as it did when Jesus was suspended between heaven and earth.

No Wonder They Call Him the Savior, p. 162

Therefore I will give him a portion among the great, and he will divide the spoils with the strong, because he poured out his life unto death, and was numbered with the transgressors.

Isaiah 53:12

MARCH 21

*C*rossbeam. Sign. Ground. Nails. Pound. Pound. Pound. Pierced. Contorted. Thirst. Terrible. Grace. Writhing. Raised. Mounted. Hung. Suspended. Spasms. Heaving. Sarcasm. Sponge. Tears. Taunts. Forgiveness. Dice. Gambling. Darkness.... Earthquake. Cemetery.

NO WONDER THEY CALL HIM THE SAVIOR, PP. 114,115

He himself bore our sins in his body on the tree, so that we might die to sins and live for righteousness; by his wounds you have been healed.

1 PETER 2:24

OCTOBER 12

The Apostle Paul said, "the wages of sin is death." He didn't say, "The wages of sin is a bad mood." Or, "The wages of sin is a hard day." Nor, "The wages of sin is depression." Read it again. "The wages of sin is death." Sin is fatal.

SIX HOURS ONE FRIDAY, P. 84

For the wages of sin is death, but the gift of God is eternal life in Christ Jesus our Lord.

ROMANS 6:23

MARCH 22

Spices. Linen. Tomb. Fear. Waiting. Despair. Stone. Mary. Running. Maybe? Peter. John. Belief. Enlightenment. Truth. Mankind. Alive. Alive. Alive!

NO WONDER THEY CALL HIM THE SAVIOR, P. 115

What I received I passed on to you as of first importance: that Christ died for our sins according to the Scriptures, that he was buried, that he was raised on the third day according to the Scriptures.

1 CORINTHIANS 15:3,4

OCTOBER 11

Thanks to all of you who practice on Monday what you hear on Sunday. You spend selfless hours with orphans, at typewriters, in board meetings, on knees, in hospital wards, away from families, and on assembly lines. It is upon the back of your fidelity that the gospel rides.

GOD CAME NEAR, P. 67

You too are being built together to become a dwelling in which God lives by his Spirit.

EPHESIANS 2:22

MARCH 23

Mary began to pour. Over his head. Over his shoulder. Down his back. She would have poured herself out for him if she could. The fragrance rushed through the room. Smells of cooked lamb and herbs were lost in the sweet ointment. "Wherever you go," the gesture spoke, "breathe the aroma and remember one who cares."

AND THE ANGELS WERE SILENT

While he was in Bethany...a woman came with an alabaster jar of very expensive perfume, made of pure nard. She broke the jar and poured the perfume on his head.

MARK 14:3

OCTOBER 10

Cries for help muffled behind costumed faces. Fear hidden behind a painted smile. Signals of desperation thought to be signs of joy. Tell me that doesn't describe our world.

SIX HOURS ONE FRIDAY, P. 208

Let us examine our ways and test them, and let us return to the Lord.

LAMENTATIONS 3:40

MARCH 24

etween the lashings, I wonder, did he relive the moment? As he hugged the Roman post and braced himself for the next ripping of his back, did he feel the oil [that Mary had poured out on him] run over his skin? Could he, in the faces of the women who stared, see the small, soft face of Mary, who cared?

AND THE ANGELS WERE SILENT

Many women were there, watching from a distance. They had followed Jesus from Galilee to care for his needs.

MATTHEW 27:55

OCTOBER 9

God is the father pacing the porch. His eyes are wide with his quest. His heart is heavy. He seeks his prodigal. He searches the horizon, he examines the skyline; yearning for the familiar figure, the recognizable gait. His concern is not his business, his investments, his owning. His concern is the son who wears his name, the child who bears his image. You. He wants you home.

And the Angels Were Silent

But while he was still a long way off, his father saw him.

Luke 15:20

MARCH 25

Final acts. Final hours. Final words. They reflect a life well-lived. So do the last words of our Master. When on the edge of death, Jesus, too, got his house in order: A final prayer of forgiveness. A plea honored.

NO WONDER THEY CALL HIM THE SAVIOR, P. 20

Jesus said, "Father, forgive them, for they do not know what they are doing." And they divided up his clothes by casting lots.... Jesus answered [his fellow victim], "I tell you the truth, today you will be with me in paradise."

LUKE 23:34,43

OCTOBER 8

Have you been called to go out on a limb for God? You can bet it won't be easy. Limb-climbing has never been easy.... Ask Jesus. He knows better than anyone the cost of hanging on a tree.

GOD CAME NEAR, P. 21

If anyone would come after me, he must deny himself and take up his cross daily and follow me.

LUKE 9:23

MARCH 26

Final acts. Final hours. Final words. They reflect a life well-lived. So do the last words of our Master. When on the edge of death, Jesus, too, got his house in order: A confession of humanity. A cry of completion.

No Wonder They Call Him the Savior, p. 20

Jesus said, "I am thirsty...." When he had received the drink, Jesus said, "It is finished." With that, he bowed his head and gave up his spirit.

John 19:28,30

OCTOBER 7

Maybe, if you had your way, your day would never end. Every moment demands to be savored. You resist sleep as long as possible because you love being awake so much. If you are like that, congratulations. If not, welcome to the majority.

SIX HOURS ONE FRIDAY, P. 30

This is the day the Lord has made; let us rejoice and be glad in it.

PSALM 118:24

MARCH 27

F inal acts. Final hours. Final words. They reflect a life well-lived. So do the last words of our Master. When on the edge of death, Jesus, too, got his house in order: A question of suffering. A call of deliverance.

No Wonder They Call Him the Savior, p. 20

Jesus cried out in a loud voice..."My God, my God, why have you forsaken me?..." "Father, into your hands I commit my spirit." When he had said this, he breathed his last.

Mark 15:34; Luke 23:46

OCTOBER 6

Flattery is nothing more than fancy dishonesty. It wasn't used by Jesus, nor should it be used by his followers.

AND THE ANGELS WERE SILENT

May the LORD cut off all flattering lips and every boastful tongue.

PSALM 12:3

MARCH 28

The Omnipotent, in one instant, made himself breakable. He who had been spirit became pierceable. He who was larger than the universe became an embryo.

GOD CAME NEAR, P. 12

Who, being in very nature God, did not consider equality with God something to be grasped, but made himself nothing, taking the very nature of a servant, being made in human likeness.

PHILIPPIANS 2:6,7

OCTOBER 5

When words are most empty, tears are most apt. A tearstain on a letter says much more than the sum of all its words. A tear falling on a casket says what a spoken farewell never could. What summons a mother's compassion and concern more quickly than a tear on a child's cheek? What gives more support than a sympathetic tear on the face of a friend?

NO WONDER THEY CALL HIM THE SAVIOR, P. 106

On his arrival, Jesus found that Lazarus had already been in the tomb for four days.... Jesus wept. Then the Jews said, "See how he loved him!"

JOHN 11:17,35,36

MARCH 29

Maybe the cross was why Jesus so loved children. They represented the very thing he would have to give: Life.

GOD CAME NEAR, P. 39

Let the little children come to me, and do not hinder them, for the kingdom of heaven belongs to such as these.

MATTHEW 19:14

GOD CAME NEAR

OCTOBER 4

What does the LORD require of you? To act justly and to love mercy and to walk humbly with your God.

MICAH 6:8

Complicated religion wasn't made by God.

AND THE ANGELS WERE SILENT

MARCH 30

Had Jesus been forced to nail himself to the cross, he would have done it. For it was not the soldiers who killed him, nor the screams of the mob: It was his devotion to us.

GOD CAME NEAR, P. 40

I lay down my life.... No one takes it from me, but I lay it down of my own accord.

JOHN 10:17,18

OCTOBER 3

Where there is opportunity for love, there is opportunity for hurt. When betrayal comes what do you do? Get out? Get angry? Get even? You have to deal with it some way. How? Begin by noticing how Jesus saw Judas. Jesus answered, "Friend, do what you came to do."

AND THE ANGELS WERE SILENT

As soon as Judas took the bread, Satan entered into him. "What you are about to do, do quickly," Jesus told him.

JOHN 13:27

MARCH 31

Can you imagine the cry from the cross? The sky is dark. The other two victims are moaning.... Perhaps there is thunder. Perhaps there is weeping. Perhaps there is silence. Then Jesus draws in a deep breath, pushes his feet down on that Roman nail, and cries, "It is finished!" What was finished? The history-long plan of redeeming man was finished. The sting of death had been removed. It was over.

NO WONDER THEY CALL HIM THE SAVIOR, P. 61

Jesus said, "It is finished." With that, he bowed his head and gave up his spirit.

JOHN 19:30

OCTOBER 2

W hy do we do what we do? Why do we take blatantly black-and-white and paint it gray? Why are priceless mores trashed while senseless standards are obeyed? What causes us to elevate the body and degrade the soul? What causes us to pamper the skin while we pollute the heart? Our values are messed up.

No Wonder They Call Him the Savior, p. 33

Buy the truth and do not sell it; get wisdom, discipline and understanding.

Proverbs 23:23

APRIL 1

Here Joseph had taught him how to grip a hammer. And on this work bench he had built his first chair. I wonder what Jesus thought as he took one last look around the room.... I wonder if he hesitated. I wonder if his heart was torn. I wonder if he rolled a nail between his thumb and fingers, anticipating the pain.

GOD CAME NEAR, P. 24

[Jesus] went down to Nazareth with [Joseph and Mary] and was obedient to them.

LUKE 2:51

OCTOBER 1

God used (and uses!) people to change the world. People! Not saints or superhumans or geniuses, but people. Crooks, creeps, lovers, and liars—he uses them all. And what they may lack in perfection, God makes up for in love.

NO WONDER THEY CALL HIM THE SAVIOR, P. 119

Do you not know that the wicked will not inherit the kingdom of God?... And that is what some of you were. But you were washed, you were sanctified, you were justified in the name of the Lord Jesus Christ and by the Spirit of our God.

1 CORINTHIANS 6:9,11

APRIL 2

A witness could not help but ask: Jesus, do you give no thought to saving yourself? What keeps you there? What holds you to the cross? Nails don't hold gods to trees. What makes you stay?

SIX HOURS ONE FRIDAY, P. 23

When it hurts to do what's right, remember Jesus.

SEPTEMBER 30

Be careful about—Denial of Christ: Whoever disowns me before men, I will disown him before my Father in heaven (Matthew 10:33). The lack of parental discipline: Do not withhold discipline from a child; if you punish him with the rod, he will not die. Punish him with the rod and save his soul from death (Proverbs 23:13,14).

GOD CAME NEAR, P. 63

APRIL 3

A t the ninth hour Jesus cried out in a loud voice…"My God, my God, why have you forsaken me?"

MARK 15:34

"My God, my God, why have you forsaken me?" The words ricochet from star to star, crashing into the chamber of the King…. The King is silent. It is the hour for which he has planned. He knows his course of action. He has awaited those words since the beginning—since the first poison was smuggled into the kingdom.

SIX HOURS ONE FRIDAY, P. 98

SEPTEMBER 29

B e careful about—Dust-covered Bibles: We must pay more careful attention, therefore, to what we have heard, so that we do not drift away (Hebrews 2:1). The poisoning effect of gossip: The words of a gossip are like choice morsels; they go down to a man's inmost parts (Proverbs 26:22).

GOD CAME NEAR, P. 63

APRIL 4

Slowly the words that would kill the Son began to come from the lips of the Father, "Hour of death, moment of sacrifice, it is your moment.... Soldiers, you think you lead him? Ropes, you think you bind him? Men, you think you sentence him? He heeds not your commands. He winces not at your lashes. It is my voice he obeys. It is my condemnation he dreads. And it is your souls he saves."

SIX HOURS ONE FRIDAY, P. 102

Pilate said, "Don't you realize I have power either to free you or to crucify you?" Jesus answered, "You would have no power over me if it were not given to you from above."

JOHN 19:10,11

SEPTEMBER 28

Be careful about—Sticking your nose in other people's business: Like one who seizes a dog by the ears is a passer-by who meddles in a quarrel not his own (Proverbs 26:17). Careless choice of companions: Bad company corrupts good character (1 Corinthians 15:33).

GOD CAME NEAR, P. 63

APRIL 5

From the lips of the Father.... "Oh, my Son, my child. Look up into the heavens and see my face before I turn it. Hear my voice before I silence it. Would that I could save you and them. But they don't see and they don't hear. The living must die so that the dying can live. The time has come to kill the Lamb. Here is the cup, my Son. The cup of sorrows. The cup of sin."

SIX HOURS ONE FRIDAY, P. 102

Father, if you are willing, take this cup from me; yet not my will, but yours be done.

LUKE 22:42

SEPTEMBER 27

The trueness of one's belief is revealed in pain. Genuineness and character are unveiled in misfortune. Faith is at its best, not in three-piece suits on Sunday mornings or at V.B.S. on summer days, but at hospital bedsides, cancer wards, and cemeteries.

NO WONDER THEY CALL HIM THE SAVIOR, P. 77

Though he slay me, yet will I trust in him.

JOB 13:15 KJV

APRIL 6

The King turns away from his Prince. The undiluted wrath of a sin-hating Father falls upon his sin-filled Son. The fire envelops him. The shadow hides him. The Son looks for his Father, but his Father cannot be seen.

SIX HOURS ONE FRIDAY, P. 103

And so Jesus also suffered outside the city gate to make the people holy through his own blood.

HEBREWS 13:12

SEPTEMBER 26

Jesus' message is just as powerful today as it was then. Don't miss it: "There is a time for risky love. There is a time for extravagant gestures. There is a time to pour out your affections on one you love. And when the time comes—seize it, don't miss it."

AND THE ANGELS WERE SILENT

Live a life of love, just as Christ loved us and gave himself up for us as a fragrant offering and sacrifice to God.

COLOSSIANS 1:8

APRIL 7

Jesus planned his own sacrifice. Jesus intentionally planted the tree from which his cross would be carved. He willingly placed the iron ore in the heart of the earth from which the nails would be cast. He voluntarily placed Judas in the womb of a woman. He didn't have to do it—but he did.

GOD CAME NEAR, P. 39

Yet it was the LORD's will to crush him and cause him to suffer.

ISAIAH 53:10

SEPTEMBER 25

I myself will be the shepherd of my sheep, and cause them to lie down in peace, the Lord God says. I will seek my lost ones, those who strayed away, and bring them safely home again.

EZEKIEL 34:15,16 TLB

God is tireless, relentless. He refuses to quit.

AND THE ANGELS WERE SILENT

APRIL 8

I t was the third hour when they crucified him.... And at the ninth hour Jesus cried out in a loud voice.

MARK 15:25,34

Those six hours were no normal six hours. They were the most critical hours in history. For during those six hours on that Friday, God embedded in the earth three anchor points sturdy enough to withstand any hurricane. Anchor point 1—My life is not futile. Anchor point 2—My failures are not fatal. Anchor point 3—My death is not final.

SIX HOURS ONE FRIDAY, P. 25

SEPTEMBER 24

G ratitude. More aware of what you have than what you don't. Recognizing the treasure in the simple—a child's hug, fertile soil, a golden sunset. Relishing in the comfort of the common— a warm bed, a hot meal, a clean shirt.

SIX HOURS ONE FRIDAY, P. 65

I have learned to be content whatever the circumstances.

PHILIPPIANS 4:11

APRIL 9

Anchor deep, say a prayer, and hold on. And don't be surprised if someone walks across the water to give you a hand.

SIX HOURS ONE FRIDAY, PP. 25,26

We have this hope as an anchor for the soul, firm and secure.

HEBREWS 6:19

SEPTEMBER 23

B ut God demonstrates his own love for us in this: While we were still sinners, Christ died for us.

ROMANS 5:8

"I love you, but I'll love you even more if..." Christ's love had none of this. No strings, no expectations, no hidden agendas, no secrets. His love for us was, and is, up front and clear. "I love you," he says. "Even if you let me down. I love you in spite of your failures."

NO WONDER THEY CALL HIM THE SAVIOR, P. 156

APRIL 10

The cross did what sacrificed lambs could not do. It erased our sins, not for a year, but for eternity.

No Wonder They Call Him the Savior, p. 140

He did not enter by means of the blood of goats and calves; but he entered the Most Holy Place once for all by his own blood.

Hebrews 9:12

SEPTEMBER 22

The invisible God had drawn near to Abraham to make his immovable promise: "To your descendants I give this land." And though God's people often forgot their God, God didn't forget them. He kept his word. The land became theirs. God didn't give up. He never gives up.

SIX HOURS ONE FRIDAY, P. 189

By faith Abraham, even though he was past age—and Sarah herself was barren—was enabled to become a father because he considered him faithful who had made the promise.

HEBREWS 11:11

APRIL 11

The next time that obnoxious neighbor Doubt walks in, escort him out. Out to the hill. Out to Calvary. Out to the cross where, with holy blood, the hand that carried the flame wrote the promise, "God would give up his only son before he'd give up on you."

SIX HOURS ONE FRIDAY, P. 190

Therefore, there is now no condemnation for those who are in Christ Jesus, because through Christ Jesus the law of the Spirit of life set me free from the law of sin and death.

ROMANS 8:1,2

SEPTEMBER 21

Jesus was the only man to walk God's earth who claimed to have an answer for man's burdens.

SIX HOURS ONE FRIDAY, P. 33

Jesus said, "Peace I leave with you; my peace I give you. I do not give to you as the world gives. Do not let your hearts be troubled and do not be afraid."

JOHN 14:27

APRIL 12

Bloodstained royalty. A God with tears. A creator with a heart. God became earth's mockery to save his children.

GOD CAME NEAR, P. 16

The message of the cross is foolishness to those who are perishing, but to us who are being saved it is the power of God.

1 CORINTHIANS 1:18

SEPTEMBER 20

If God is God anywhere, he has to be God in the face of death. Pop psychology can deal with depression. Pep talks can deal with pessimism. Prosperity can handle hunger. But only God can deal with our ultimate dilemma—death.

GOD CAME NEAR, P. 33

Our Savior, Christ Jesus,...has destroyed death and has brought life and immortality to light through the gospel.

2 TIMOTHY 1:10

APRIL 13

Those who can remain...are a rare breed. I don't necessarily mean win, I just mean remain. Hang in there. Finish. Stick to it until it is done. But unfortunately, very few of us do that. Our human tendency is to quit too soon. Our human tendency is to stop before we cross the finish line.

No Wonder They Call Him the Savior, p. 60

Jesus said, "Remain in me, and I will remain in you."

John 15:4

SEPTEMBER 19

The journey will end and we will take our seat at his feast... forever. See you at the table.

AND THE ANGELS WERE SILENT

Then the angel said to me, "Write: 'Blessed are those who are invited to the wedding supper of the Lamb!'" And he added, "These are the true words of God."

REVELATION 19:9

APRIL 14

Jesus stretched his hands as open as he could. He forced his arms so wide apart that it hurt. And to prove that those arms would never fold and those hands would never close, he had them nailed open. They still are.

SIX HOURS ONE FRIDAY, P. 209

Who shall separate us from the love of Christ? Shall trouble or hardship or persecution or famine or nakedness or danger or sword? No, in all these things we are more than conquerors through him who loved us.

ROMANS 8:35,37

SEPTEMBER 18

Peace where there should be pain. Confidence in the midst of crisis. Hope defying despair. That's what that look says. It is a look that knows the answer to the question asked by every mortal: "Does death have the last word?" I can see Jesus wink as he gives the answer. "Not on your life."

SIX HOURS ONE FRIDAY, P. 225

The sting of death is sin, and the power of sin is the law. But thanks be to God! He gives us the victory through our Lord Jesus Christ.

1 CORINTHIANS 15:56,57

APRIL 15

No price is too high for a parent to pay to redeem his child. No energy is too great. No effort too demanding. A parent will go to any length to find his or her own. So will God.

AND THE ANGELS WERE SILENT

As a father has compassion on his children, so the LORD has compassion on those who fear him; for he knows how we are formed, he remembers that we are dust.

PSALM 103:13,14

SEPTEMBER 17

I t's not every day that you find someone who will give you a second chance—much less someone who will give you a second chance every day.

NO WONDER THEY CALL HIM THE SAVIOR, P. 95

If we confess our sins, he is faithful and just and will forgive us our sins and purify us from all unrighteousness.

1 JOHN 1:9

APRIL 16

Anchor points were planted firmly in bedrock two thousand years ago by a carpenter who claimed to be the Christ. And it was all done in the course of a single day. A single Friday. All done during six hours one Friday.

SIX HOURS ONE FRIDAY, P. 176

You see, at just the right time, when we were still powerless, Christ died for the ungodly.

ROMANS 5:6

SEPTEMBER 16

W hile we are talking about setting people free to fly, think about yourself. How are you at giving wings? How have you been at setting people free? That friend who offended you and needs your forgiveness? The co-worker burdened with fear of the grave? The relative who carries the sack of yesterday's failures? Tell them about the empty tomb...and watch them fly.

AND THE ANGELS WERE SILENT

How beautiful on the mountains are the feet of those who bring good news, who proclaim peace, who bring good tidings, who proclaim salvation.

ISAIAH 52:7

APRIL 17

To the casual observer the six hours are mundane...but to the handful of awestruck witnesses the most maddening of miracles is occurring. God is on a cross. The creator of the universe is being executed.... And there is no one to save him, for he is sacrificing himself.

SIX HOURS ONE FRIDAY, P. 177

For you know the grace of our Lord Jesus Christ, that though he was rich, yet for your sakes he became poor, so that you through his poverty might become rich.

2 CORINTHIANS 8:9

SEPTEMBER 15

They complained that he healed on the wrong day...forgave the wrong people...hung out with the wrong crowd and had the wrong influence on the children. But, still worse, every time he tried to set people free, the religious leaders attempted to tie them down. When a courageous soul tried to fly they were there to say it couldn't be done.

AND THE ANGELS WERE SILENT

Woe to you, teachers of the law and Pharisees, you hypocrites! You shut the kingdom of heaven in men's faces. You yourselves do not enter, nor will you let those enter who are trying to.

MATTHEW 23:13

APRIL 18

S ix hours on one Friday. Six hours that jut up on the plain of human history like Mount Everest in a desert. Six hours that have been deciphered, dissected, and debated for two thousand years. What do these six hours signify? They claim to be the door in time through which eternity entered man's darkest caverns.

SIX HOURS ONE FRIDAY, P. 170

I am the Living One; I was dead, and behold I am alive for ever and ever! And I hold the keys of death and Hades.

REVELATION 1:18

SEPTEMBER 14

Jesus may have had pimples. He may have been tone-deaf. Perhaps a girl down the street had a crush on him or vice versa. It could be that his knees were bony. One thing's for sure: He was, while completely divine, completely human.

GOD CAME NEAR, P. 12

For in Christ all the fullness of the Deity lives in bodily form.

COLOSSIANS 2:9

APRIL 19

For the life blackened with failure, that Friday means forgiveness. For the heart scarred with futility, that Friday means purpose. And for the soul looking into this side of the tunnel of death, that Friday means deliverance. What do you do with...that Friday?

SIX HOURS ONE FRIDAY, P. 171

Through him we have gained access by faith into this grace in which we now stand. And we rejoice in the hope of the glory of God.

ROMANS 5:2

SEPTEMBER 13

No doubt you've had your share of words that wound.... Maybe your wound is old. Though the arrow was extracted long ago, the arrowhead is still lodged...hidden under your skin. If you have suffered or are suffering because of someone else's words, you'll be glad to know that there is a balm for this laceration.

No Wonder They Call Him the Savior, pp. 24,25

When they hurled their insults at [Jesus], he did not retaliate; when he suffered, he made no threats. Instead, he entrusted himself to him who judges justly.

1 Peter 2:23

APRIL 20

Jesus saw you in your Garden of Gethsemane—and he didn't want you to be alone. He wanted you to know that he has been there too. He knows what it's like to be plotted against. He knows what it's like to be confused. He knows what it's like to be torn between two desires.... He knows what it's like to beg God to change his mind and to hear God say so gently, but firmly, "No."

AND THE ANGELS WERE SILENT

I desire to do your will, O my God; your law is within my heart.

PSALM 40:8

SEPTEMBER 12

What unlocked the doors of the apostles' hearts? Simple. They saw Jesus. They encountered the Christ. Their sins collided with their Savior and their Savior won! What lit the boiler of the apostles was a red-hot conviction that the very one who should have sent them to hell went to hell for them and came back to tell about it.

Six Hours One Friday, p. 73

When he ascended up on high, he led captivity captive, and gave gifts unto men.

Ephesians 4:8 KJV

APRIL 21

The torches gave just enough light for Malchus to see the flash of the sword and "swoosh!" He leans back enough to save his neck but not his ear. Peter gets a rebuke and Malchus gets a healing touch.... From that night on, whenever Malchus would hear people talk about the carpenter who rose from the dead, he wouldn't scoff. No, he'd tug at his earlobe and know that it was possible.

No Wonder They Call Him the Savior, p. 75

One of [the disciples] struck the servant of the high priest, cutting off his right ear. But Jesus answered, "No more of this!" And he touched the man's ear and healed him.

Luke 22:50,51

SEPTEMBER 11

The apostles sparked a movement. The people became followers of the death-conqueror. They couldn't hear enough or say enough about him. People began to call them "Christ-ians." Christ was their model, their message. They preached "Jesus Christ and him crucified," not for the lack of another topic, but because they couldn't exhaust this one.

SIX HOURS ONE FRIDAY, P. 73

I resolved to know nothing while I was with you except Jesus Christ and him crucified.

1 CORINTHIANS 2:2

APRIL 22

The cross, the zenith of history. All of the past pointed to it and all of the future would depend upon it.

AND THE ANGELS WERE SILENT

Just as Moses lifted up the snake in the desert, so the Son of Man must be lifted up.

JOHN 3:14

SEPTEMBER 10

Hope is not a granted wish or a favor performed; no, it is far greater than that. It is a zany, unpredictable dependence on a God who loves to surprise us out of our socks.

GOD CAME NEAR, P. 45

When [Jesus] was at the table with them, he took bread, gave thanks, broke it and began to give it to them. Then their eyes were opened and they recognized him, and he disappeared from their sight.

LUKE 24:30,31

APRIL 23

God demonstrates his own love for us in this: While we were still sinners, Christ died for us.

ROMANS 5:8

God on a cross. Humanity at its worst. Divinity at its best.

NO WONDER THEY CALL HIM THE SAVIOR, P. 162

SEPTEMBER 9

God's not a genie. He's not a good luck charm or the man upstairs. He is, instead, the creator of the universe who is right here in the thick of our day-to-day world who speaks to you more through cooing babies and hungry bellies than he ever will through horoscopes, zodiac papers, or weeping Madonnas.

AND THE ANGELS WERE SILENT

He is not served by human hands, as if he needed anything, because he himself gives all men life and breath and everything else.... so that men would seek him and perhaps reach out for him and find him, though he is not far from each one of us.

ACTS 17:25,27

APRIL 24

Quadriplegics, AIDS victims, or the terminally ill. Single parents. Alcoholics. Divorcees. The blind. All, to one degree or another, shunned by the "normal world." Society doesn't know what to do with them. And, sadly, even the church doesn't know. They often would find a warmer reception at the corner bar than in a Sunday school class. But Jesus would find a place for them.

GOD CAME NEAR, P. 29

Listen, my dear brothers: Has not God chosen those who are poor in the eyes of the world to be rich in faith and to inherit the kingdom?

JAMES 2:5

SEPTEMBER 8

Have you got God figured out? Have you got God captured on a flowchart and frozen on a flannel board? If so, then listen. Listen to God's surprises. Hear the rocks meant for the body of the adulterous woman drop to the ground.... Listen to the widow from Nain eating dinner with her son who is supposed to be dead. And listen...as Mary's name is spoken by a man she loved—a man she had buried.

SIX HOURS ONE FRIDAY, P. 162

He who was seated on the throne said, "I am making everything new!"
REVELATION 21:5

APRIL 25

A re you building any towers? Examine your motives. And remember the statement imprinted on the base of the windswept Tower of Babel: Blind ambition is a giant step away from God and one step closer to catastrophe.

GOD CAME NEAR, P. 61

Unless the LORD builds the house, its builders labor in vain.

PSALM 127:1

SEPTEMBER 7

Behind his pursuit of us is the same brilliance behind the rotating seasons and the orbiting planets. Heaven and earth know no greater passion than God's personal passion for you and your return.

AND THE ANGELS WERE SILENT

I tell you...there is more rejoicing in heaven over one sinner who repents than over ninety-nine righteous persons who do not need to repent.

LUKE 15:7

APRIL 26

Mark it down. God's greatest creation is not the flung stars or the gorged canyons, it's his eternal plan to reach his children.

<small>AND THE ANGELS WERE SILENT</small>

The unsearchable riches of Christ...this mystery, which for ages past was kept hidden in God, who created all things.

<small>EPHESIANS 3:8,9</small>

SEPTEMBER 6

Seekers of popularity, power, and pleasure. The end result is the same: painful unfulfillment. Only in seeing his Maker does a man truly become man. For in seeing his Creator man catches a glimpse of what he was intended to be.

GOD CAME NEAR, P. 46

The world and its desires pass away, but the man who does the will of God lives forever.

1 JOHN 2:17

APRIL 27

Let go of your territory for a while. Explore some new reefs. Scout some new regions. Much is gained by closing your mouth and opening your eyes.

AND THE ANGELS WERE SILENT

Even a fool is thought wise if he keeps silent, and discerning if he holds his tongue.

PROVERBS 17:28

SEPTEMBER 5

Two blind men were sitting by the roadside, and when they heard that Jesus was going by, they shouted, "Lord, Son of David, have mercy on us!"

MATTHEW 20:30

Of all the people, it is the blind who really see Jesus. Something told these two beggars that God is more concerned with the right heart than he is the right clothes or procedure. Somehow they knew that what they lacked in method could be made up for in motive, so they called out at the top of their lungs. And they were heard. God always hears those who seek him.

AND THE ANGELS WERE SILENT

APRIL 28

The best way to deal with our past is to hitch up our pants, roll up our sleeves, and face it head on. No more buck-passing or scape-goating. No more glossing over or covering up. No more games. We need a confrontation with our Master.

GOD CAME NEAR, P. 73

"Come now, let us reason together," says the LORD. "Though your sins are like scarlet, they shall be as white as snow; though they are red as crimson, they shall be like wool."

ISAIAH 1:18

SEPTEMBER 4

So close to the timber yet so far from the blood. We are so close to the world's most uncommon event, but we act like common crapshooters huddled in bickering groups and fighting over silly opinions. How many pulpit hours have been wasted on preaching the trivial?... So close to the cross but so far from the Christ.

NO WONDER THEY CALL HIM THE SAVIOR, P. 126

May I never boast except in the cross of our Lord Jesus Christ.

GALATIANS 6:14

APRIL 29

S tability in the storm comes not from seeking a new message, but from understanding an old one. The most reliable anchor points are not recent discoveries, but are time-tested truths that have held their ground against the winds of change.

SIX HOURS ONE FRIDAY, P. 174

We must pay more careful attention, therefore, to what we have heard, so that we do not drift away.

HEBREWS 2:1

SEPTEMBER 3

The younger son got together all he had, set off for a distant country and there squandered his wealth in wild living.

<small>LUKE 15:13</small>

His first few days of destitution were likely steamy with resentment. He was mad at everyone. Everyone was to blame. His friends shouldn't have bailed out on him. And his brother should come and bail him out. His boss should feed him better and his dad never should have let him go in the first place. He named a pig after each one of them.

<small>SIX HOURS ONE FRIDAY, P. 208</small>

APRIL 30

As moments go, that one appeared no different than any other.... But in reality, that particular moment was like none other. For through that segment of time a spectacular thing occurred. God became a man.

GOD CAME NEAR, P. 12

When the time had fully come, God sent his Son, born of a woman.

GALATIANS 4:4

SEPTEMBER 2

Aging? Death? Self? The next time you find yourself alone in a dark alley facing the undeniables of life, don't cover them with a blanket, or ignore them with a nervous grin. Don't turn up the TV and pretend they aren't there. Instead, stand still, whisper his name, and listen. He is nearer than you think.

GOD CAME NEAR, P. 54

Call to me and I will answer you.

JEREMIAH 33:3

MAY 1

Take heart. "Since the children have flesh and blood (that's you and me), he too shared in their humanity (that's Jesus, our big brother) so that by his death he might destroy him who holds the power of death—that is, the devil—and free those who all their lives were held in slavery by their fear of death. For surely it is not angels he helps, but Abraham's descendants (that's us)" (Hebrews 2:14-16, parentheses mine).

SIX HOURS ONE FRIDAY, P. 134

SEPTEMBER 1

Jesus thought worship was more important than work?... Such is the purpose of the Sabbath. And such was the practice of Jesus.... If Jesus found time in the midst of a racing agenda to stop the rush and sit in the silence, do you think we could, too?

AND THE ANGELS WERE SILENT

He went to Nazareth, where he had been brought up, and on the Sabbath day he went into the synagogue, as was his custom.

LUKE 4:16

MAY 2

Jesus' invitation is clear and non-negotiable. He gives all and we give him all. Simple and absolute. He is clear in what he asks and clear in what he offers. The choice is up to us.

<small>AND THE ANGELS WERE SILENT</small>

I am the bread of life. He who comes to me will never go hungry, and he who believes in me will never be thirsty.

<small>JOHN 6:35</small>

AUGUST 31

We can choose where we spend eternity. The big choice God leaves to us. The critical decision is ours. What are you doing with God's invitation? What are you doing with his personal request that you live with him forever?

AND THE ANGELS WERE SILENT

Everyone who calls on the name of the Lord will be saved.

ROMANS 10:13

MAY 3

God doesn't remember my mistakes. For all the things he does do, this is one thing he refuses to do. He refuses to keep a list of my wrongs. When I ask for forgiveness he doesn't pull out a clipboard and say, "But I've already forgiven him for that five hundred and sixteen times." He doesn't remember.

GOD CAME NEAR, P. 50

I will forgive their wickedness and will remember their sins no more.

HEBREWS 8:12

AUGUST 30

W hat we already have is far greater than anything we might want.

SIX HOURS ONE FRIDAY, P. 68

I consider everything a loss compared to the surpassing greatness of knowing Christ Jesus my Lord, for whose sake I have lost all things. I consider them rubbish, that I may gain Christ.

PHILIPPIANS 3:8

MAY 4

A man is never the same after he simultaneously sees his utter despair and Christ's unbending grace. To see the despair without the grace is suicidal. To see the grace without the despair is...futility. But to see them both is conversion.

SIX HOURS ONE FRIDAY, P. 77

Godly sorrow brings repentance that leads to salvation and leaves no regret, but worldly sorrow brings death.

2 CORINTHIANS 7:10

AUGUST 29

There is not a hint of one person who was afraid to draw near Jesus. There were those who mocked him. There were those who were envious of him. There were those who misunderstood him. There were those who revered him. But there was not one person who considered him too holy, too divine, or too celestial to touch. There was not one person who was reluctant to approach him for fear of being rejected.

GOD CAME NEAR, P. 27

Jesus said, "Whoever comes to me I will never drive away."

JOHN 6:37

May 5

What good has hatred ever brought? What hope has anger ever created? What problems have ever been resolved by revenge?

No Wonder They Call Him the Savior, p. 28

When they hurled their insults at [Jesus], he did not retaliate; when he suffered, he made no threats. Instead, he entrusted himself to him who judges justly.

1 Peter 2:23

AUGUST 28

I f you are looking for my prediction of the day Christ will return, sorry. You won't find it here. He hasn't chosen to give us that date, so time spent speculating is time poorly used. He has chosen, however, to give a manual of survival for lives under siege.

AND THE ANGELS WERE SILENT

The Son of Man will come at an hour when you do not expect him.

LUKE 12:40

MAY 6

Are you so seldom in one place that your friends regard you as a phantom? Are you so constantly on the move that your family is beginning to question your existence? Do you take pride in your frenzy at the expense of your faith?

AND THE ANGELS WERE SILENT

Man is a mere phantom as he goes to and fro: He bustles about, but only in vain; he heaps up wealth, not knowing who will get it.

PSALM 39:6

AUGUST 27

We didn't make the alcohol, but our highways have drunk drivers. We don't sell drugs, but our neighborhoods have those who do. We didn't create international tension, but we have to fear the terrorists. We didn't train the thieves, but each of us is a potential victim of their greed. We are tiptoeing through a mine field which we didn't create.

AND THE ANGELS WERE SILENT

I have told you these things, so that in me you may have peace. In this world you will have trouble. But take heart! I have overcome the world.

JOHN 16:33

MAY 7

If there was anything that Jesus wanted everyone to understand it was this: A person is worth something simply because he is a person. That is why he treated people like he did. Think about it. The girl caught making undercover thunder with someone she shouldn't—he forgave her. The untouchable leper who asked for cleansing—he touched him.

No Wonder They Call Him the Savior, p. 35

You are precious and honored in my sight, and...I love you.

Isaiah 43:4

GOD CAME NEAR

AUGUST 26

My failures are not fatal. It's not that he loves what you did, but he loves who you are. You are his. The one who has the right to condemn you provided the way to acquit you. You make mistakes. God doesn't. And he made you.

SIX HOURS ONE FRIDAY, P. 25

The LORD appeared to us in the past, saying: "I have loved you with an everlasting love."

JEREMIAH 31:3

MAY 8

Questions for Mary: What was it like watching Jesus pray? Did you ever feel awkward teaching him how he created the world? Did you ever scold him? Did you ever think: That's God eating my soup?

GOD CAME NEAR, PP. 18,19

Then [Jesus] went down to Nazareth with [Mary and Joseph] and was obedient to them.

LUKE 2:51

AUGUST 25

We can't help but wonder: What if? What if Pilate had come to the defense of the innocent? What if Herod had asked Jesus for help and not entertainment? What if the High Priest had been as concerned with truth as he was his position? What if one of them had turned their back on the crowd and their face toward the Christ and made a stand? But they didn't.

AND THE ANGELS WERE SILENT

For they loved praise from men more than praise from God.

JOHN 12:43

MAY 9

More questions for Mary: When Jesus saw a rainbow, did he ever mention a flood? How did he act at funerals? Did he ever come home with a black eye? What did he and his cousin John talk about as kids? Did you ever accidently call him Father?

GOD CAME NEAR, PP. 18,19

[Jesus] grew and became strong; he was filled with wisdom, and the grace of God was upon him.

LUKE 2:40

AUGUST 24

R eliability. It's the bread and butter characteristic of achievement. It's the shared ingredient behind retirement pens, Hall of Fame awards, and golden anniversaries. It is the quality that produces not momentary heroics but monumental lives.

GOD CAME NEAR, P. 66

The things you have heard me say in the presence of many witnesses entrust to reliable men who will also be qualified to teach others.

2 TIMOTHY 2:2

MAY 10

And though God's people often forgot their God, God didn't forget them. He kept his word.... He never gives up. When Joseph was dropped into a pit by his own brothers, God didn't give up. When Moses said, "Here I am, send Aaron," God didn't give up. When the delivered Israelites wanted Egyptian slavery instead of milk and honey, God didn't give up.

SIX HOURS ONE FRIDAY, P. 57

If we are faithless, he will remain faithful, for he cannot disown himself.

2 TIMOTHY 2:13

AUGUST 23

God, with eyes twinkling, steps up to the philosopher's blackboard, erases the never-ending, ever-repeating circle of history and replaces it with a line; a hope-filled, promising, slender line. And, looking over his shoulder to see if the class is watching, he draws an arrow on the end. In God's book man is heading somewhere.

NO WONDER THEY CALL HIM THE SAVIOR, PP. 34,35

Faith and love...spring from the hope that is stored up for you in heaven and that you have already heard about in the word of truth, the gospel.

COLOSSIANS 1:5

JULY 2

Pride is made of stone. Hard knocks may chip it, but it takes reality's sledgehammer to break it.

Six Hours One Friday, p. 208

Pride goes before destruction, a haughty spirit before a fall.

PROVERBS 16:18

JULY 1

Quit trying to quench your own guilt. You can't do it. There's no way. Not with a bottle of whiskey or perfect Sunday School attendance. Sorry. I don't care how bad you are. You can't be bad enough to forget it. And I don't care how good you are. You can't be good enough to overcome it. You need a Savior.

No Wonder They Call Him the Savior, pp. 140,141

All of us have become like one who is unclean, and all our righteous acts are like filthy rags.

Isaiah 64:6

JULY 3

God's testimony. When was the last time you witnessed it? A stroll through knee-high grass in a green meadow. An hour listening to seagulls or looking at seashells on the beach. Or witnessing the shafts of sunlight brighten the snow on a crisp winter dawn. Miracles that almost match the magnitude of the empty tomb happen all around us; we only have to pay attention.

NO WONDER THEY CALL HIM THE SAVIOR, P. 147

The heavens declare the glory of God; the skies proclaim the work of his hands.

PSALM 19:1

JUNE 30

On earth, Jesus was an artist in a gallery of his own paintings. He was a composer listening as the orchestra interpreted his music. He was a poet hearing his own poetry. Yet his works of art had been defaced. Creation after battered creation. He had created people for splendor.

SIX HOURS ONE FRIDAY, P. 93

We are God's workmanship, created in Christ Jesus to do good works, which God prepared in advance for us to do.

EPHESIANS 2:10

JULY 4

The LORD is in his holy temple; the LORD is on his heavenly throne. He observes the sons of men; his eyes examine them.... For the LORD is righteous, he loves justice.

PSALM 11:4,7

God will do what is right, every time.

AND THE ANGELS WERE SILENT

JUNE 29

I keep thinking of all the people who cast despairing eyes toward the dark heavens and cry, "Why?" And I imagine Jesus. I imagine him listening. I picture his eyes misting and a pierced hand brushing away a tear. And although he may offer no answer, although he may solve no dilemma, although the question may freeze painfully in mid-air, he who also was once alone, understands.

No Wonder They Call Him the Savior, p. 48

For we do not have a high priest who is unable to sympathize with our weaknesses, but we have one who has been tempted in every way, just as we are—yet was without sin.

Hebrews 4:15

JULY 5

W ant to anger God? Get in the way of people who want to see him. Want to feel his fury? Exploit people in the name of God. Mark it down. Religious hucksters poke the fire of divine wrath.

AND THE ANGELS WERE SILENT

Jesus entered the temple area and drove out all who were buying and selling there. He overturned the tables of the money changers and the benches of those selling doves. "It is written," he said to them, "'My house will be called a house of prayer,' but you are making it a 'den of robbers.'"

MATTHEW 21:12,13

JUNE 28

It is more than Jesus can take.... He watched in silence as those he loved ran away. He did not retaliate when the insults were hurled, nor did he scream when the nails pierced his wrists. But when God turned his head, that was more than he could handle. "My God!" The wail rises from parched lips. The holy heart is broken. "Why? Why did you abandon me?" I can't understand it. I honestly cannot. Why did Jesus do it?

No Wonder They Call Him the Savior, p. 48

Surely he took up our infirmities and carried our sorrows, yet we considered him stricken by God, smitten by him, and afflicted.

Isaiah 53:4

JULY 6

Science and statistics wave their unmagic wand across the face of life, squelching the oohs and aahs and replacing them with formulas and figures. Would you like to see Jesus? Do you dare be an eyewitness of His Majesty? Then rediscover amazement. The next time you hear a baby laugh or see an ocean wave, take note. Pause and listen as His Majesty whispers ever so gently, "I'm here."

GOD CAME NEAR, P. 43

We were eyewitnesses of his majesty. For he received honor and glory from God the Father.

2 PETER 1:16,17

JUNE 27

Tomorrow's joy is fathered by today's acceptance. Acceptance of what, at least for the moment, you cannot alter.

GOD CAME NEAR, P. 71

I have learned to be content whatever the circumstances.

PHILIPPIANS 4:11

JULY 7

To see Jesus, go to the community hospital and ask the nurse to take you to see one who has received no visits. To see Jesus, leave your office and go down the hall and talk to the man who is regretting his divorce and missing his children.... To see Jesus...see the unattractive and forgotten.

AND THE ANGELS WERE SILENT

Jesus said, "The Spirit of the Lord is on me, because he has anointed me to preach good news to the poor. He has sent me to proclaim freedom for the prisoners and recovery of sight for the blind, to release the oppressed."

LUKE 4:18

JUNE 26

You can tell a lot about a person by the way they die. And the way Jesus marched to his death leaves no doubt: he had come to earth for this moment.

AND THE ANGELS WERE SILENT

Now my heart is troubled, and what shall I say? "Father, save me from this hour"? No, it was for this very reason I came to this hour. Father, glorify your name!

JOHN 12:27,28

JULY 8

Pilgrims with no vision of the promised land become proprietors of their own land. They set up camp. They exchange hiking boots for loafers and trade in their staff for a new recliner.

GOD CAME NEAR, PP. 78,79

Here we do not have an enduring city, but we are looking for the city that is to come.

HEBREWS 13:14

JUNE 25

God comes to your house, steps up to the door and knocks. But it's up to you to let him in.

AND THE ANGELS WERE SILENT

Here I am! I stand at the door and knock. If anyone hears my voice and opens the door, I will come in and eat with him, and he with me.

REVELATION 3:20

JULY 9

S low down. If God commanded rest, you need it. If Jesus modeled it, you need it. God still provides the manna. Trust him. Take a day to say "no" to work and "yes" to worship.

AND THE ANGELS WERE SILENT

Because so many people were coming and going that they did not even have a chance to eat, [Jesus] said to them, "Come with me by yourselves to a quiet place and get some rest."

MARK 6:31

JUNE 24

You won't look at anyone else. No side glances to see what others are wearing. No whispers about new jewelry or comments about who is present. At this, the greatest gathering in history, you will have eyes for only one—the Son of Man. Wrapped in splendor. Shot through with radiance. Imploded with light and magnetic in power.

<small>AND THE ANGELS WERE SILENT</small>

When the Son of Man comes in his glory, and all the angels with him, he will sit on his throne in heavenly glory.

<small>MATTHEW 25:31</small>

JULY 10

What God did makes sense. It makes sense that Jesus would be our sacrifice.... However, why God did it is absolutely absurd.... That type of love isn't logical; it can't be neatly outlined in a sermon or explained in a term paper.

GOD CAME NEAR, P. 15

When we were God's enemies, we were reconciled to him through the death of his Son.

ROMANS 5:10

JUNE 23

An eternal instant. A moment that reminds you of the treasures surrounding you. Your home. Your peace of mind. Your health. A moment that tenderly rebukes you for spending so much time on temporal preoccupations such as savings accounts, houses, and punctuality. A moment that can bring a mist to the manliest of eyes and perspective to the darkest life.

GOD CAME NEAR, P. 41

For what shall it profit a man, if he shall gain the whole world, and lose his own soul?

MARK 8:36 KJV

JULY 11

Y ou are tired. You are weary. Weary of being slapped by the waves of broken dreams. Weary of being stepped on and run over in the endless marathon to the top. Weary of trusting in someone only to have that trust returned in an envelope with no return address.

SIX HOURS ONE FRIDAY, P. 179

He gives strength to the weary and increases the power of the weak.

ISAIAH 40:29

JUNE 22

To put a lock and key on your emotions is to bury part of your Christ-likeness! Especially when you come to Calvary. You can't go to the cross with just your head and not your heart. It doesn't work that way. Calvary is not a mental trip.... It's a heart-splitting hour of emotion.... Look again. Those are nails in those hands. That's God on that cross. It's us who put him there.

No Wonder They Call Him the Savior, p. 108

Rend your heart and not your garments. Return to the LORD your God, for he is gracious and compassionate.

Joel 2:13

JULY 12

Jesus was the only man to walk God's earth who claimed to have an answer for man's burdens. "Come to me," he invited them. My prayer is that you, too, will find rest.

Six Hours One Friday, p. 179

Come to me, all you who are weary and burdened, and I will give you rest. Take my yoke upon you and learn from me...and you will find rest for your souls.

Matthew 11:28,29

JUNE 21

Jesus wears a sovereign crown but bears a father's heart. He is a king who writes tender notes to his children asking them to come home. A king who can't rest until he is sure his children are safe. A king who would die to get his family home.

AND THE ANGELS WERE SILENT

He who watches over you will not slumber; indeed, he...will neither slumber nor sleep.

PSALM 121:3,4

GOD CAME NEAR

JULY 13

W hat do you do with a man who claims to be God, yet hates religion? What do you do with a man who calls himself the Savior, yet condemns systems? What do you do with a man who knows the place and time of his death, yet goes there anyway?

AND THE ANGELS WERE SILENT

Who has known the mind of the Lord? Or who has been his counselor?

ROMANS 11:34

JUNE 20

R each up and take your Father's hand and say what my daughter Andrea said to me, "I'm not sure where I am. I'm not sure which is the road home. But you do and that's enough."

<small>AND THE ANGELS WERE SILENT</small>

For I am the Lord, your God, who takes hold of your right hand and says to you, Do not fear; I will help you.

<small>ISAIAH 41:13</small>

JULY 14

Insensitive comments. Thoughts that should have remained thoughts. Feelings which had no business being expressed.... He who dares to call himself God's ambassador is not afforded the luxury of idle words. Excuses such as, "I didn't know you were here," or, "I didn't realize this was so touchy," are shallow when they come from those who claim to be followers and imitators of the Great Physician.

GOD CAME NEAR, PP. 68,69

Set a guard over my mouth, O LORD; keep watch over the door of my lips.

PSALM 141:3

JUNE 19

From the first time a father reaches to take his daughter's infant hand, she reaches up and takes his heart. She never returns it. He is her protector, her provider. Her knight. Her hero. In turn she is his lamb. His angel on loan. His beauty of beauties.

And the Angels Were Silent

He tends his flock like a shepherd: He gathers the lambs in his arms and carries them close to his heart.

Isaiah 40:11

JULY 15

Those tiny drops of humanity. Those round, wet balls of fluid that tumble from our eyes, creep down our cheeks, and splash on the floor our hearts.... They are miniature messengers, on call twenty-four hours a day to substitute for crippled words. They drip, drop, and pour from the corner of our souls, carrying with them the deepest emotions we possess.

No Wonder They Call Him the Savior, p. 106

Jesus wept.

John 11:35 KJV

JUNE 18

My father taught me how to shave and how to pray. He helped me memorize verses for Sunday school and taught me that wrong should be punished and that rightness has its own reward. He modeled the importance of getting up early and staying out of debt. His life expressed the elusive balance between ambition and self-acceptance.

GOD CAME NEAR, P. 64

Listen to your father, who gave you life.

PROVERBS 23:22

JULY 16

W hen God chose to reveal himself, he did so (surprise of surprises) through a human body. The tongue that called forth the dead was a human one. The hand that touched the leper had dirt under its nails. The feet upon which the woman wept were calloused and dusty. And his tears...oh, don't miss the tears...they came from a heart as broken as yours or mine ever has been.

GOD CAME NEAR, P. 27

The Father, living in me...is doing his work.

JOHN 14:10

JUNE 17

M y father didn't do anything unusual. He only did what dads are supposed to do—be there.

GOD CAME NEAR, P. 64

A father to the fatherless, a defender of widows, is God in his holy dwelling.

PSALM 68:5

JULY 17

N oah's God is your God. The promise given to Abram is given to you. The finger witnessed in Pharaoh's world is moving in yours. God is in the thick of things in your world. He has not taken up residence in a distant galaxy. He has not removed himself from history. He has not chosen to seclude himself on a throne in an incandescent castle.

AND THE ANGELS WERE SILENT

The eyes of the LORD range throughout the earth to strengthen those whose hearts are fully committed to him.

2 CHRONICLES 16:9

JUNE 16

Father's Day. A day of cologne. A day of hugs, new neckties, long-distance telephone calls, and Hallmark cards. Today is my first Father's Day without a father. For thirty-one years I had one. I had one of the best. But now he's gone. He's buried under an oak tree in a West Texas cemetery. Even though he's gone, his presence is very near—especially today.

GOD CAME NEAR, P. 64

The righteous man leads a blameless life; blessed are his children after him.

PROVERBS 20:7

JULY 18

Jesus said, "It is finished." With that, he bowed his head and gave up his spirit.

JOHN 19:30

Words of chance muttered by a desperate martyr? No. Words of intent, painted by the Divine Deliverer on the canvas of sacrifice.

NO WONDER THEY CALL HIM THE SAVIOR, P. 21

JUNE 15

Joseph had to push away the sheep and clear out the cow patties so his wife would have a place to give birth. He became a fugitive of the law. He spent two years trying to understand Egyptian.... He never regretted it. Sweet was the reward for his courage. One look in the face of that heavenly toddler and he knew he would do it again in a heartbeat.

GOD CAME NEAR, P. 21

When Joseph woke up, he did what the angel of the Lord had commanded him and took Mary home as his wife. But he had no union with her until she gave birth to a son.

MATTHEW 1:24,25

JULY 19

Jesus said, "The Sabbath was made for man, not man for the Sabbath."

MARK 2:27

Keep a clear vision of the cross on your horizon and you can find your way home. Such is the purpose of your day of rest: to relax your body, but more importantly, to restore your vision...a day in which you get your bearings so you can find your way home.

AND THE ANGELS WERE SILENT

JUNE 14

Value is now measured by two criteria—appearance and performance. Pretty tough system, isn't it? Where does that leave the retarded? Or the ugly or uneducated? Where does that place the aged or the handicapped? What hope does that offer the unborn child? Not much. Not much at all. We become nameless numbers on mislaid lists. Now please understand, this is man's value system. It is not God's.

No Wonder They Call Him the Savior, p. 34

He hath made us accepted in the Beloved.

Ephesians 1:6 KJV

JULY 20

He who would see his God would then see the reason for death and the purpose of time.

GOD CAME NEAR, P. 46

The fear of the LORD is the beginning of wisdom, and knowledge of the Holy One is understanding.

PROVERBS 9:10

JUNE 13

R ather than shocking the globe with an occasional demonstration of deity, God has opted to display his power daily. Proverbially. Pounding waves. Prism-cast colors. Birth, death, life. We are surrounded by miracles. God is throwing testimonies at us like fireworks, each one exploding, "God is! God is!"

GOD CAME NEAR, P. 42

Since the creation of the world God's invisible qualities—his eternal power and divine nature—have been clearly seen.

ROMANS 1:20

JULY 21

Jesus wept. He wept not for the dead but for the living. He wept not for the one in the cave of death but for those in the cave of fear. He wept for those who, though alive, were dead. He wept for those who, though free, were prisoners, held captive by their fear of death.

SIX HOURS ONE FRIDAY, P. 228

On his arrival, Jesus found that Lazarus had already been in the tomb for four days.... Jesus wept.

JOHN 11:17,35

JUNE 12

The price of practicality is sometimes higher than extravagance. But the rewards of risky love are always greater than its cost.

AND THE ANGELS WERE SILENT

Love the Lord your God with all your heart and with all your soul and with all your strength.

DEUTERONOMY 6:5

JULY 22

We are free either to love God or not. He invites us to love him. He urges us to love him. He came that we might love him. But, in the end, the choice is yours and mine. To take that choice from each of us, for him to force us to love him, would be less than love.... In the end, he leaves the choice with us.

AND THE ANGELS WERE SILENT

On the last and greatest day of the Feast, Jesus stood and said in a loud voice, "If anyone is thirsty, let him come to me and drink."

JOHN 7:37

JUNE 11

You see, the message is hard to believe. We insist on making God one of us. We persist in casting him with human attributes. We tell ourselves: No person loves me that much, so certainly God doesn't love me that much. No one could forgive that mistake, so certainly God couldn't. If my parents who brought me here don't care, how can I expect God to?

AND THE ANGELS WERE SILENT

The LORD appeared to us in the past, saying: "I have loved you with an everlasting love; I have drawn you with loving-kindness."

JEREMIAH 31:3

JULY 23

Hell was not prepared for people. Hell was "prepared for the devil and his angels" (Matthew 25:41). For a person to go to hell, then, is for a person to go against God's intended destiny.... Hell is man's choice, not God's choice.

AND THE ANGELS WERE SILENT

God did not appoint us to suffer wrath but to receive salvation through our Lord Jesus Christ.

1 THESSALONIANS 5:9

JUNE 10

J esus. The man. The bronzed Galilean who spoke with such thunderous authority and loved with such childlike humility. The God. The one who claimed to be older than time and greater than death.

GOD CAME NEAR, P. 6

"I tell you the truth," Jesus answered, "before Abraham was born, I am!"

JOHN 8:58

JULY 24

H is Majesty. The emperor of Judah. The soaring eagle of eternity. The noble admiral of the Kingdom. All the splendor of heaven revealed in a human body.

GOD CAME NEAR, P. 7

We have seen his glory, the glory of the one and only Son, who came from the Father, full of grace and truth.

JOHN 1:14

JUNE 9

The Cross did what man could not do. It granted us the right to talk with, love, and even live with God.

NO WONDER THEY CALL HIM THE SAVIOR, P. 140

God did this so that men would seek him and perhaps reach out for him and find him, though he is not far from each one of us.

ACTS 17:27

JULY 25

Jesus said, "If you believe, you will receive whatever you ask for in prayer."

MATTHEW 21:22

Don't reduce this grand statement to the category of new cars and paychecks. Don't limit the promise of this passage to the selfish pool of perks and favors. The fruit God assures is far greater than earthly wealth. His dreams are much greater than promotions and proposals. God wants you to fly.

AND THE ANGELS WERE SILENT

JUNE 8

Father forgive them, for they do not know what they are doing.

LUKE 23:34

Have you ever asked how Jesus kept his control? Here's the answer. It's the second part of his statement.... It's as if Jesus considered this bloodthirsty, death-hungry crowd not as murderers, but as victims. It's as if he saw in their faces not hatred but confusion. It's as if he regarded them not as a militant mob but, as he put it, as "sheep without a shepherd." "They don't know what they are doing."

NO WONDER THEY CALL HIM THE SAVIOR, P. 29

JULY 26

Calvary is a hybrid of God's lofty status and his deep devotion. The thunderclap which echoed when God's sovereignty collided with his love. The marriage of heaven's kingship and heaven's compassion. The very instrument of the cross is symbolic, the vertical beam of holiness intersecting the horizontal bar of love.

AND THE ANGELS WERE SILENT

God was pleased to have all his fullness dwell in him, and through him to reconcile to himself all things, whether things on earth or things in heaven, by making peace through his blood, shed on the cross.

COLOSSIANS 1:19,20

JUNE 7

Think about the first time you ever saw Jesus. Think about your first encounter with the Christ. Robe yourself in that moment. Resurrect the relief. Recall the purity. Summon forth the passion. Can you remember?

SIX HOURS ONE FRIDAY, P. 196

Create in me a pure heart, O God, and renew a steadfast spirit within me.... Restore to me the joy of your salvation.

PSALM 51:10,12

JULY 27

A braham let the word get out that Sarah wasn't his wife but his sister. Can you build a nation on that kind of faith? God can.... Moses. Would you choose a wanted murderer to lead a nation out of bondage? God did.... Gomer, the prostitute; Sarah, the woman who giggled at God. One story after another of God using man's best and overcoming man's worst.

No Wonder They Call Him the Savior, pp. 117-119

We have this treasure in jars of clay to show that this all-surpassing power is from God and not from us.

2 Corinthians 4:7

JUNE 6

braham, or Abram as he was known at the time, was finding God's promise about as easy to swallow as a chicken bone. The promise? That his descendants would be as numerous as the stars. The problem? No son. "No problem," came God's response. Abraham looked over at his wife Sarah as she shuffled by in her gown and slippers with the aid of a walker. The chicken bone stuck.

Six Hours One Friday, p. 55

Abraham fell facedown; he laughed and said to himself, "Will a son be born to a man a hundred years old? Will Sarah bear a child at the age of ninety?"

Genesis 17:17

JULY 28

The people God used to change history: A ragbag of ne'er-do-wells and has-beens who found hope, not in their performance, but in God's proverbially open arms.

No Wonder They Call Him the Savior, p. 117

God chose the foolish things of the world to shame the wise; God chose the weak things of the world to shame the strong.

1 Corinthians 1:27

JUNE 5

A n hour of contentment. An hour when deadlines are forgotten and strivings have ceased. An hour when what we have overshadows what we want. An hour when we realize that a lifetime of blood-sweating and headhunting can't give us what the cross gave us in one day—a clean conscience and a new start.

No Wonder They Call Him the Savior, p. 121

Godliness with contentment is great gain.

1 Timothy 6:6

JULY 29

My life is not futile.... There is truth. Someone is in control and I have a purpose.

SIX HOURS ONE FRIDAY, P. 25

The LORD will fulfill his purpose for me; your love, O LORD, endures forever.

PSALM 138:8

J U N E 4

R eliable servants. They're the binding of the Bible. Their acts are rarely recited and their names are seldom mentioned. Yet were it not for their loyal devotion to God, many great events never would have occurred.

God Came Near, p. 66

And what more shall I say? for the time would fail me to tell of Gideon, and of Barak, and of Samson, and of Jephtha...of whom the world was not worthy.

Hebrews 11:32,38 KJV

JULY 30

S ee, the Lord is coming with thousands upon thousands of his holy ones to judge everyone.

JUDE 1:14

Every person who has ever lived will be present at that final gathering. Every heart that has ever beat. Every mouth that has ever spoken. On that day you will be surrounded by a sea of people. Rich, poor. Famous, unknown. Kings, bums. Brilliant, demented. All will be present. And all will be looking in one direction. All will be looking at him.

AND THE ANGELS WERE SILENT

JUNE 3

The father's loyalty to Jesus is the Father's loyalty to you. When you feel betrayed remember that.... When all of earth turns against you, all of heaven turns toward you.

AND THE ANGELS WERE SILENT

God has said, "Never will I leave you; never will I forsake you."

HEBREWS 13:5

JULY 31

It wasn't an act of impulse. She'd carried the large vial of perfume from her house to Simon's. It wasn't a spontaneous gesture. But it was an extravagant one. The perfume was worth a year's wages. Maybe the only thing of value she had. It wasn't a logical thing to do, but since when has love been led by logic?

AND THE ANGELS WERE SILENT

Mary took about a pint of pure nard, an expensive perfume; she poured it on Jesus' feet and wiped his feet with her hair. And the house was filled with the fragrance of the perfume.

JOHN 12:3

JUNE 2

God is the housewife in search of the lost coin. No matter that he has nine others. He won't rest until he has found the tenth. He searches the house. He moves furniture. He pulls up rugs. He cleans out the shelves. He stays up late. He gets up early. All other tasks can wait. Only one matters. The coin is of great value to him. He owns it. He will not stop until he finds it. The coin he seeks is you.

AND THE ANGELS WERE SILENT

Suppose a woman has ten silver coins and loses one. Does she not light a lamp, sweep the house and search carefully until she finds it?

LUKE 15:8

AUGUST 1

I n your Bible of over a thousand pages, what matters? Among all the do's and don'ts and should's and shouldn'ts, what is essential? What is indispensable? The Old Testament? The New? Grace? Baptism?... The part that matters is the cross. No more and no less. The cross.

NO WONDER THEY CALL HIM THE SAVIOR, PP. 12,13

But God forbid that I should glory, save in the cross of our Lord Jesus Christ.

GALATIANS 6:14 KJV

JUNE 1

The battle is won. You may have thought it was won on Golgotha. It wasn't. You may have thought the sign of victory is the empty tomb. It isn't. The final battle was won in Gethsemane. And the sign of conquest is Jesus at peace in the olive trees. For it was in the garden that he made his decision. He would rather go to hell for you than go to heaven without you.

AND THE ANGELS WERE SILENT

He went away a second time and prayed, "My Father, if it is not possible for this cup to be taken away unless I drink it, may your will be done."

MATTHEW 26:42

AUGUST 2

aithful servants have a way of knowing answered prayer when they see it, and a way of not giving up when they don't.

GOD CAME NEAR, P. 67

Jesus told his disciples...that they should always pray and not give up.
LUKE 18:1

MAY 31

Destiny? Tomorrow? Truth? All are questions within the reach of the man who knows his source. It is in seeing Jesus that man sees his Source.

GOD CAME NEAR, P. 46

For in him we live and move and have our being.

ACTS 17:28

AUGUST 3

Y ou have two choices. You can reject Jesus. That is an option. You can, as have many, decide that the idea of God becoming a carpenter is too bizarre—and walk away. Or you can accept him. You can journey with him. You can listen for his voice amidst the hundreds of voices and follow him.

AND THE ANGELS WERE SILENT

But blessed are your eyes because they see, and your ears because they hear.

MATTHEW 13:16

GOD CAME NEAR

MAY 30

My face looked at me from the shiny marble. It reminded me that I, too, have been dying as long as I have been living. I, too, will someday have my named carved in a granite stone. Someday I, too, will face death.

SIX HOURS ONE FRIDAY, P. 218

As for man, his days are like grass, he flourishes like a flower of the field; the wind blows over it and it is gone.... But from everlasting to everlasting the Lord's love is with those who fear him.

PSALM 103:16,17

AUGUST 4

O h, for the attitude of a five-year-old! That simple uncluttered passion for living that can't wait for tomorrow. A philosophy of life that reads, "Play hard, laugh hard, and leave the worries to your father." A bottomless well of optimism flooded by a perpetual spring of faith. Is it any wonder Jesus said we must have the heart of a child before we can enter the kingdom of heaven?

AND THE ANGELS WERE SILENT

Jesus said, "I tell you the truth, unless you change and become like little children, you will never enter the kingdom of heaven."

MATTHEW 18:3

MAY 29

Do you believe that God is near? He wants you to. He wants you to know that he is in the midst of your world. Wherever you are as you read these words, he is present. In your car. On the plane. In your office, your bedroom, your den. He's near. And he is more than near. He is active.

AND THE ANGELS WERE SILENT

"How can I give you up?... My heart is changed within me; all my compassion is aroused. I am God, and not man—the Holy One among you."

HOSEA 11:8,9

AUGUST 5

Had any visits from Doubt lately? If you find yourself going to church in order to be saved and not because you are saved, then you've been listening to him. If you find yourself doubting if God could forgive you again for that, you've been sold some snake oil. If you are more cynical about Christians than sincere about Christ, then guess who came to dinner.

SIX HOURS ONE FRIDAY, P. 189

When he asks, he must believe and not doubt, because he who doubts is like a wave of the sea, blown and tossed by the wind.

JAMES 1:6

MAY 28

Someone convinced us that the human race is headed nowhere. That man has no destiny. That we are in a cycle. That there is no reason or rhyme to this absurd existence. Somewhere we got the idea that the earth is just a spinning mausoleum and the universe is purposeless. The creation was incidental and humanity has no direction.

No Wonder They Call Him the Savior, p. 33

"I know the plans I have for you," declares the Lord, "plans to prosper you and not to harm you, plans to give you hope and a future."

Jeremiah 29:11

AUGUST 6

When the disciples were together, with the doors locked for fear of the Jews, Jesus came and stood among them and said, "Peace be with you!"

JOHN 20:19

The stone of the tomb was not enough to keep Jesus in. The walls of the room were not enough to keep him out.

SIX HOURS ONE FRIDAY, P. 72

MAY 27

God has drawn near. He has involved himself in the car pools, heartbreaks, and funeral homes of our day. He is as near to us on Monday as on Sunday. In the school room as in the sanctuary. At the coffee break as at the communion table. Why? Why did God do it? What was his reason?

AND THE ANGELS WERE SILENT

How precious to me are your thoughts, O God! How vast is the sum of them! Were I to count them, they would outnumber the grains of sand.

PSALM 139:17,18

AUGUST 7

W e live in an art gallery of divine creativity and yet are content to gaze only at the carpet.

GOD CAME NEAR, P. 42

We are bringing you good news, telling you to turn from these worthless things to the living God, who made heaven and earth and sea and everything in them.... He has not left himself without testimony.

ACTS 14:15,17

MAY 26

God doesn't just forgive, he forgets. He erases the board. He destroys the evidence. He burns the microfilm. He clears the computer.

GOD CAME NEAR, P. 50

As far as the east is from the west, so far has he removed our transgressions from us.

PSALM 103:12

AUGUST 8

Until you are able to call your enemy your friend, a jail door is closed and a prisoner is taken. But when you open the door and release your foe from your hatred, then the prisoner is released and that prisoner is you.

AND THE ANGELS WERE SILENT

Jesus said, "If you do not forgive men their sins, your Father will not forgive your sins."

MATTHEW 6:15

MAY 25

The teachers of the law and the Pharisees brought in a woman caught in adultery. They...said to Jesus, "Teacher, this woman was caught in the act of adultery. In the Law Moses commanded us to stone such women. Now what do you say?"

JOHN 8:3-5

In her despair the woman looks at the Teacher. His eyes don't glare. "Don't worry," they whisper, "it's okay." And for the first time that morning she sees kindness.... How could she ever forget those eyes? Clear and tear-filled. Eyes that saw her not as she was, but as she was intended to be.

SIX HOURS ONE FRIDAY, PP. 202,203

AUGUST 9

Now listen, you who say, "Today or tomorrow we will go to this or that city, spend a year there, carry on business and make money." Why, you do not even know what will happen tomorrow.

JAMES 4:13,14

"Someday, I will have time to call and chat." "Someday, the children will understand why I was so busy." But you know the truth, don't you? You know even before I write it. You could say it better than I. Someday never comes.

AND THE ANGELS WERE SILENT

MAY 24

O ur task on earth is singular—to choose our eternal home. You can afford many wrong choices in life. You can choose the wrong career and survive, the wrong city and survive, the wrong house and survive. You can even choose the wrong mate and survive. But there is one choice that must be made correctly, and that is your eternal destiny.

AND THE ANGELS WERE SILENT

What good is it for a man to gain the whole world, and yet lose or forfeit his very self?

LUKE 9:25

AUGUST 10

The next time you use the phrase "just a moment,..." remember that's all the time it will take to change this world.

GOD CAME NEAR, P. 13

We shall all be changed, in a moment, in the twinkling of an eye, at the last trump: for the trumpet shall sound, and the dead shall be raised incorruptible, and we shall be changed.

1 CORINTHIANS 15:51,52 KJV

MAY 23

After three years of ministry, hundreds of miles, thousands of miracles, innumerable teachings, Jesus asks who. Jesus bids the people to ponder not what he has done but who he is. It's the ultimate question of the Christ: Whose son is he?

AND THE ANGELS WERE SILENT

Jesus said, "What do you think about the Christ? Whose son is he?"

MATTHEW 22:42

AUGUST 11

D on't we see that the beauty of God is that he does what we can't? Can't we understand that where people fail God succeeds? Isn't the message of Christmas and Easter and all of the Bible that what is impossible with man is possible with God? What man can't do, God does.

AND THE ANGELS WERE SILENT

With man this is impossible, but not with God; all things are possible with God.

MARK 10:27

MAY 22

To limit God's revelation to a cold list of do's and don'ts is as tragic as looking at a Colorado road map and saying that you'd seen the Rockies.

GOD CAME NEAR, P. 27

The thief comes only to steal and kill and destroy; I have come that they may have life, and have it to the full.

JOHN 10:10

AUGUST 12

O ne. One church. One faith. One Lord. Not Baptist, not Methodist, not Adventist. Just Christians. No denominations. No hierarchies. No traditions. Just Christ. Too idealistic? Impossible to achieve? I don't think so.... Once upon a tree, a Creator gave his life for his creation. Maybe all we need are a few hearts.... What about you? Can you build a bridge?

NO WONDER THEY CALL HIM THE SAVIOR, P. 127

There is one body and one Spirit—just as you were called to one hope when you were called—one Lord, one faith, one baptism; one God and Father of all, who is over all and through all and in all.

EPHESIANS 4:4-6

MAY 21

Jesus doesn't say, "If you succeed you will be saved." Or, "If you come out on top you will be saved." He says, "If you endure." An accurate rendering would be, "If you hang in there until the end...if you go the distance."

AND THE ANGELS WERE SILENT

He who stands firm to the end will be saved.

MATTHEW 24:13

AUGUST 13

J esus told her, "Go, call your husband and come back." "I have no
husband," she replied.

JOHN 4:16,17

You've wanted to take off your mask. You've wanted to stop pretending.
You've wondered what God would do if you opened your cobweb-
covered door of secret sin. This woman wondered what Jesus would
do. She must have wondered if the kindness would cease when the
truth was revealed. *He will be angry.... He will think I'm worthless....*
No. It wasn't perfection that Jesus was seeking, it was honesty.

SIX HOURS ONE FRIDAY, P. 40

MAY 20

It may surprise you that Jesus made preparedness the theme of his last sermon. It did me. I would have preached on love or family or the importance of church. Jesus didn't. Jesus preached on what many today consider to be old-fashioned. He preached on being ready for heaven and staying out of hell.

AND THE ANGELS WERE SILENT

Keep watch, because you do not know on what day your Lord will come.

MATTHEW 24:42

AUGUST 14

Jesus said, "I tell you the truth, anyone who gives you a cup of water in my name because you belong to Christ will certainly not lose his reward."

MARK 9:41

When we do good things to others we do good things to God.

AND THE ANGELS WERE SILENT

MAY 19

What if each face were a billboard that announced the true state of its owner's heart? How many would say, "Desperate! Business on the Rocks!" or, "Broken: In Need of Repair," or, "Faithless, Frantic, and Fearful"?

GOD CAME NEAR, P. 71

Nothing in all creation is hidden from God's sight. Everything is uncovered and laid bare before the eyes of him to whom we must give account.

HEBREWS 4:13

AUGUST 15

Make an investment in the people the world has cast off—the homeless, the AIDS patient, the orphan, the divorcee—and you may discover the source of your independence. Jesus' message is stirring: the way you treat them is the way you treat me.

AND THE ANGELS WERE SILENT

The King will reply, "I tell you the truth, whatever you did for one of the least of these brothers of mine, you did for me."

MATTHEW 25:40

MAY 18

A nd when you think about it, they didn't. They hadn't the faintest idea what they were doing. They were a stir-crazy mob, mad at something they couldn't see so they took it out on, of all people, God.

NO WONDER THEY CALL HIM THE SAVIOR, P. 29

Jesus said, "Father, forgive them, for they do not know what they are doing."

LUKE 23:34

AUGUST 16

God always rejoices when we dare to dream. In fact, we are much like God when we dream. The Master exults in newness. He delights in stretching the old. He wrote the book on making the impossible possible.

AND THE ANGELS WERE SILENT

Jesus said, "Everything is possible for him who believes."

MARK 9:23

MAY 17

The church of Jesus Christ began with a group of frightened men in a second-floor room in Jerusalem.... The one betrayed sought his betrayers. What did Jesus say to them? Not, "What a bunch of flops!" Not, "I told you so." No "Where-were-you-when-I-needed-you?" speeches. But simply one phrase, "Peace be with you." The very thing they didn't have was the very thing he offered: peace.

SIX HOURS ONE FRIDAY, P. 195

A week later his disciples were in the house again.... Though the doors were locked, Jesus came and stood among them and said, "Peace be with you!"

JOHN 20:26

AUGUST 17

J esus said, "As the Father has sent me, I am sending you."

JOHN 20:21

It all started with ten stammering, stuttering men.... And send them he did. Ports. Courtyards. Boats. Synagogues. Prisons. Palaces. They went everywhere. Their message of the Nazarene dominoed across the civilized world. They were an infectious fever. They were a moving organism. They refused to be stopped. Uneducated drifters who shook history like a housewife shakes a rug.

NO WONDER THEY CALL HIM THE SAVIOR, PP. 163,164

MAY 16

Funerals, divorces, illnesses, and stays in the hospital—you can't lie about life at such times. Maybe that's why Jesus is always present at such moments.

GOD CAME NEAR, P. 54

Surely I am with you always, to the very end of the age.

MATTHEW 28:20

AUGUST 18

God is not stumped by an evil world. He doesn't gasp in amazement at the dearth of our faith or the depth of our failures. We can't surprise God with our cruelties. He knows the condition of the world...and loves it just the same. For just when we find a place where God would never be (like on a cross), we look again and there he is, in the flesh.

NO WONDER THEY CALL HIM THE SAVIOR, P. 162

In him we have redemption through his blood, the forgiveness of sins, in accordance with the riches of God's grace.

EPHESIANS 1:7

MAY 15

Jesus is honest about the life we are called to lead. There is no guarantee that just because we belong to him we will go unscathed. No promise is found in Scripture that says when you follow the king you are exempt from battle.

AND THE ANGELS WERE SILENT

I have told you these things, so that in me you may have peace. In this world you will have trouble. But take heart! I have overcome the world.

JOHN 16:33

AUGUST 19

L ife wasted pacing up and down in a self-made cell of fear. It is shocking. It is tragic. It is a pity. And it is also very common.

SIX HOURS ONE FRIDAY, P. 228

For God hath not given us the spirit of fear; but of power, and of love, and of a sound mind.

2 TIMOTHY 1:7 KJV

MAY 14

Go to the effort. Invest the time. Write the letter. Make the apology. Take the trip. Purchase the gift. Do it. The seized opportunity renders joy. The neglected brings regret.

AND THE ANGELS WERE SILENT

But encourage one another daily, as long as it is called Today.

HEBREWS 3:13

AUGUST 20

If we are not teaching people how to be saved, it is perhaps because we have forgotten the tragedy of being lost! If we're not teaching the message of forgiveness, it may be because we don't remember what it was like to be guilty. And if we're not preaching the cross, it could be that we've subconsciously decided that—God forbid—somehow we don't need it.

SIX HOURS ONE FRIDAY, P. 196

For Christ [sent] me to preach the gospel—not with words of human wisdom, lest the cross of Christ be emptied of its power.

1 CORINTHIANS 1:17

MAY 13

Lie still, tiny mouth. Lie still, mouth from which eternity will speak. Tiny tongue that will soon summon the dead, that will define grace, that will silence our foolishness. Rosebud lips—upon which ride a starborn kiss of forgiveness to those who believe you, and of death to those who deny you—lie still.

GOD CAME NEAR, P. 17

Then Simeon blessed them and said to Mary, [Jesus'] mother: "This child is destined to cause the falling and rising of many in Israel."

LUKE 2:34

AUGUST 21

I will forgive their wickedness and will remember their sins no more.

HEBREWS 8:12

Do you think God was teasing when he said that? Was he exaggerating when he said he would cast our sins as far as the east is from the west? Do you actually believe he would make a statement like, "I will not hold their iniquities against them," and then rub our noses in them whenever we ask for help? Of course you don't. You and I just need an occasional reminder of God's nature, his forgetful nature.

GOD CAME NEAR, P. 51

GOD CAME NEAR

MAY 12

Rest well, tiny hands. For though you belong to a king, you will touch no satin, own no gold. You will grasp no pen, guide no brush. No, your tiny hands are reserved for works more precious: to touch a leper's open wound, to wipe a widow's weary tear, to claw the ground of Gethsemane.

GOD CAME NEAR, P. 17

[Mary] gave birth to her firstborn, a son. She wrapped him in cloths and placed him in a manger.

LUKE 2:7

AUGUST 22

D ays come and go. Seasons ebb and flow. Every sunrise which becomes a sunset whispers the secret, "Time will take your sandcastles."

AND THE ANGELS WERE SILENT

Command those who are rich in this present world not to be arrogant nor to put their hope in wealth, which is so uncertain, but to put their hope in God.

1 TIMOTHY 6:17

MAY 11

When God became flesh and was the victim of an assassination attempt before he was two years old, he didn't give up. When the people from his own home town tried to push him over a cliff, he didn't give up. When his brothers ridiculed him, he didn't give up. When he was accused of blaspheming God by people who didn't fear God, he didn't give up.... God would give up his only son before he'd give up on you.

SIX HOURS ONE FRIDAY, PP. 58,59

God so loved the world that he gave his one and only Son, that whoever believes in him shall not perish, but have eternal life.

JOHN 3:16